WHAT IS THE TRUTH?

MC JOHNSTON

WHAT IS THE TRUTH?

I AM THE WAY, THE TRUTH AND THE LIFE

GOD WANTS NONE TO PERISH

TATE PUBLISHING
AND ENTERPRISES, LLC

Published by Tate Publishing & Enterprises, LLC
127 E. Trade Center Terrace | Mustang, Oklahoma 73064 USA
1.888.361.9473 | www.tatepublishing.com

Tate Publishing is committed to excellence in the publishing industry. The company reflects the philosophy established by the founders, based on Psalm 68:11,
"The Lord gave the word and great was the company of those who published it."

Book design copyright © 2013 by Tate Publishing, LLC. All rights reserved.
Cover design by Joel Uber
Interior design by Jomar Ouano

Published in the United States of America

ISBN: 978-1-62510-625-4
Religion / Biblical Studies / General
13.07.15

DEDICATION

To all those who were and will be saved by the Sinner's Prayer.

To my daughters, Christine, Cynthia, Cassandra, Clarissa, Carla and

To all my grandchildren, great-grandchildren and families

To God having made known unto us the mystery of his will, according to his good pleasure which he purposed in himself: that in the dispensation of the fullness of times he might gather together in one all things in Christ, both which are in heaven, and which are on earth; even in him: in whom also we have obtained an inheritance, being predestinated according to the purpose of him who works all things after the counsel of his own will: That we *should* be to the praise of his glory, who first trusted in Christ. Ephesians 1:9-12 (KJV)

PROLOGUE

My Name is

Lord Jesus Christ

Son of the Living God

Sent To Fulfill

The Reconciliation Between

God and Man

God's Mystery Accomplished!

Read and Learn

What is The Truth?

CONTENTS

PREFACE

Change is something that irritates most people and yet there seems to be a change of something about every hour. Technology began so that people would take life easier and spend more time with their family and friends. Somehow the changes began to backfire and people had to work harder and longer. This is the twenty-first century and we have cell phones that are computers, TV, radio, camera, bank and many more things. They are all old within months. Work that was once nine to five and forty hours a week, have become rare today. Work hours are much longer and now most are a two working family. Our government is working to change America into the rest of the third world countries so we will fit into the one world government. The Democrats and Republicans have also betrayed us; the only ones that can see our freedoms disappearing are the Tea Party Americans. We can't really call them conservatives, because half of them are against the Tea Party. We started with swords and then guns, then Tommy-guns, now we are up to bombs and nuclear missiles. The coming down of America is causing people to stress, which cause sickness, which seems to be the only thing to slow people down. We have all forgotten that there really is an end to this maddening world and we still continue to ask: "What is Truth?"

Believe it or not, It actually has been put into perspective thinking today, such as:

When the earth is turned away from the sun, there is an absence of heat, which is called cold.

Perspective thinking is: Cold is the absence of heat.

Again, as the earth is turned away from the sun, there is an absence of light, which is called darkness.

Perspective thinking is: darkness is the absence of light.

When people turn away from doing good, there is an absence of goodness, which is called sinful.

Perspective thinking is: People committing sin is the absence of people doing good.

Further perspective thinking is: GOD is known for his goodness and yet there is an absence of many doing good. But there is much sinning, which is known by the Evil ones-evil world.

Perspective thinking is: Sinning from the evil one's sinful world is the absence of knowing God and his goodness.

Perspective thinking is: Those who know the good GOD will be with him always in Heaven and those that are absence of the good GOD will be forever with the Evil one, which is called Hell.

The good news is that the good GOD sent his only begotten Son to die on the cross for our sins and he rose again. Those who choose to believe this truth of Jesus Christ the Son of GOD, Son of man, He will also give us life and we will rise again to heaven and live forever with the good GOD.

When you make your choice, keep eternal life in mind, it is forever. Either place is eternal but only one is good and the other is torment. The good GOD had never intended for his human children to go to hell. It was only for fallen angels and demons but man chose self-power and disobeyed the good GOD.

So, Who Are We? How did we get here anyway? How do we get out of here?

WHO ARE WE?

We are sinners born into a dark world of sin and death and destruction, and many of us have come to believe that we belong here. But it is not unusual, if we are born sinners, our nature would be to sin. Even if we tried to change that, the Evil one of this world is the king of all sinners and would be there to help us change our minds. Entertainment and addictive things and sex are the enticements of this dark world. Sinners are naturally self-centered and selfish and can never be satisfied. We have no desire to have anyone around that would disagree with us. We know what we want and we will do what we must to make sure that we get it. So be careful not to push us too far because we can get very angry and may even get out of control.

Then people began to turn to the evil one and to commit every sin the evil one enticed. Sinners are capable of becoming, thieves and liars, adulterers, fornicators and murderers. It is in the hearts of all sinners and God searches all hearts. And if we do those things, the god of sin and death will come and try to steal our good thoughts, and try to kill us or destroy us or just hope that we will kill ourselves.

Which brings up the question: Why would the god of the world of sin and death want to kill people that are just like himself? Why would he hate us and do these evil things to us. He is the ruler of this fallen world and he wants to take everyone he can away from God; and doesn't want us to see the light and get saved, then he is no longer our king.

And how did we get here anyway?

HOW DID WE GET HERE?

What if I was to tell you that this was a perfect world, where we would be joyful, never be confused, never get overwhelmed, no stress, never get sick, never get hurt, never get angry and never die? I'm sure there are many more things that a loving Father would want to give His children.

What if, right now, we would be able to find the way into this perfect world? Almost sounds like a fairytale, doesn't it? Most would say, "Too good to be true," then many would say, "but knowing the truth will set you free."

What if I was to tell you that once upon a time before the world of sin and death, there was a perfect world and a heavenly Father who had two children, called Adam and Eve? What if, the Father had created the whole planet Earth full of living things and set it into a fantastic, gorgeous and functional universe? And on the Earth He planted a beautiful garden that would supply them with everything they could possibly need. They would work in the garden and care for all the animals and in the evening the Father would spend time with them. All was so perfect and the Father loved them so much that the he gave them the deed to rule over all living things on the earth. There was only one thing that was asked of them in return for such a paradise. The Holy Father's word was truth and He said, "You may eat of all the trees in the garden except the one in the midst, the tree of the knowledge of good and evil, for if you eat of that tree you will surely die." They were both created with the knowledge of good but also with a free will to choose the righteousness of the Father or the knowledge of evil. So as long as they obeyed, life was good and that was all they knew or needed to know.

What if a fallen cherubim came to them in the form of a serpent and spoke lies to God's children and they forgot that their Holy Father's word was truth and they believed the lies? The serpent deceived them by saying that, "You shall not surely die. For God knows that if you eat the fruit, then your eyes will be opened and you shall be as gods." This had been the desire of the fallen angel who was called Satan or the devil. They chose to eat the fruit of the tree of the knowledge of good and evil. Their eyes were opened and they had changed and saw themselves naked and had the same fear of the Father as the serpent. The Father asked, Where are you? Adam said that he hid because he was afraid and was naked. Because of their unbelief of the Fathers word and their disobedience, the god of sin and death was able to take the deed from the children and become the ruler of the now fallen world. The children had died spiritually on the inside but not physically. By giving the deed to the devil they had defiled all that the Father had created and because sin is so evil that it would take the shedding of innocent blood to cover it. The Father killed an innocent animal and shed its blood into the ground to cover their sin and made them a covering of skins for their nakedness. He would have to send them out of the garden before they could eat of the tree of life and remain in a sinful state forever. God gave Adam and Eve and the devil, the curses that they brought upon themselves. From that day forward all children born through the seed of Adam would be born sinners. It would take an innocent human male that was born of a woman; but not with the seed of Adam, but who could shed innocent blood to pay for the sins of the fallen world. This would be an impossible task with no hope for the children to go back to the garden. Who could ever qualify or desire to die and save us from this fallen world?

HOW DO WE GET OUT OF HERE?

What if, the Holy Father had made a plan to get all his children back without having to deal with our sin nature? It has been longsuffering plans watching us make many mistakes and as time pasted many of the fallen children of the world forgot the Holy Father. Many, because we did not want to give up the only way we knew to live; but our self-centered sin nature would continue to grow more evil. Many of us would be ignorant to the fact that we truly are ruled by the god of the world of sin and death and would do the things, which would please the devil. The god of the world is able to blind our minds from the light of the Father's truth. That would deceive us so we would not believe the truth but believe the lies that we hear. "There is a way, which seems right unto a man, but the end thereof are the ways of death" (Pr 14:12).

It would not be an easy task for a Holy Father of righteousness and truth to deal with the evil paths his children would take. It is also very difficult for the children with a free will in a fallen world to choose to live good lives when the pleasures of the world seem so enticing. Love and redemption of his children is always foremost on the Father's mind and he does have a way to escape evil and begin a new life with him.

JESUS CHRIST IS GOING TO SAVE THE WORLD:

He who hears the Gospel (Jesus died and was buried and in three days he arose again from the dead); and chooses to believe, shall be saved. For God so loved the world that he gave his only begotten Son, that whosoever believes in him should not perish, but have everlasting life. God sent not his Son into the world to condemn the world, but that the world through him might be saved.

HOW WILL HE DO IT?

1   By revealing the nature of the true good God of love through Jesus Christ.

2   By fulfilling all of God's Word that spoke of the Messiah, even the suffering Messiah that was written by the prophets and the Law of Moses.

3   By shedding his own innocent blood, dying on the cross and by his resurrection from the dead, he takes sin out of the way and destroying the works of the devil.

4   By taking sin out of the way so God could have His longsuffering desire to reconcile into his love relationship with his begotten children for all eternity.

5   By teaching after the resurrection how Israel would be on hold while the New Testament, which is The Age

of Grace is fulfilled and Saints hold the inheritance of Eternal Redemption and Eternal Life (knowing God).

God has given us his Word (Bible) to show us his love and teaches us with the help of the Holy Spirit, how to prepare ourselves for Heaven. It is a process of building a relationship with the Creator of the Universe through Jesus Christ.

WHAT DO WE NEED TO DO?

Declare from your heart that you are sinner and need a savior to save you. Jesus Christ is the only innocent man with no sin. Ask him to be your Lord and Savior and that Christ may dwell in your hearts by faith; that you, being rooted and grounded in love, and he will give you eternal life in Him. But Jesus Christ said, "We must be born again, born of water and Spirit."

Time is very close for us who desire to be saved from sin and death; receive your salvation and when you leave this fallen world you can take your proper place with the Father forever.

You will see in the remainder of this book how the love of the Holy Father has made a quest to redeem his fallen children and bring us all home to everlasting life with Him.

His quest has been written in The Bible and the stories of the chosen men and women that desired to be obedient and tried to be a help to bring the Father's plan to victory. For God so loved the world (his children) that he gave his only begotten Son, that whosoever believed in him should nor perish, but have everlasting life.

This book is to show the journey of our loving God's longsuffering years that it took to bring reconciliation between God and man. I pray as God also does, that all should find and learn the mystery so none should perish, no, not one, but all be saved.

PART ONE

GOD'S HISTORICAL DISPOSITIONS

CHAPTER 1

CREATION AND THE FALL
(ADAM TO NOAH)

In the beginning God created the heaven and the earth. God created a universe and arranged them so that the earth would be central and perfectly compatible to the needs of his human children he would create. He began to see, speak, and bring into existence all of the laws of the universe and the perfect world for humans to live. He gave them light to see by and darkness to sleep by; water ways under the earth, and water above for rain. Then he divided the seas from the dry land called earth; then the earth brought forth grass, herb yielding seed after its kind, fruit yielding trees after its kind; then came the lights in the firmament of the heaven for signs, seasons, days and years; the larger light to rule the day and the lesser light to rule the night and the stars also. Then God created the great whales, and every living creature that moves in the water; and every wing fowl after his kind and God blessed them and said to be fruitful and multiply. God made the beast of the earth after his kind and every thing that creeps upon the earth after his kind. Then God said, "Let us make man in our image, after our likeness."

When God created mankind, male and female, He used all of the attributes that were in the Godhead. All are made according to where we fit in the plan of God and what attributes we will need to complete his purpose for us on the earth. Our bodies were made with great complexity and each with great purposes, the greatest being procreation. All living things on the earth were created with the ability to multiply themselves and replenish the earth. God created Adam, the male human first and Adam named all living things; seeing that each one had a helpmate but there was none for Adam. God saw the desire in his heart and put him to sleep and took a rib from him and created the female human and brought her to him. They were called the man and woman. It was intended that a man would be complete when he found a woman helpmate and there would be a mutual love cleave in marriage. God said as a prophecy for the future for the first man and woman; when they would become a mother and father, that their son would leave them and cleave to his wife: and they shall be one flesh. (*Together they would be complete but if separated, it would be much like when man fell, there would be something lost in their hearts that can only be found when rejoined; and God said "it is not good for man to be alone".*)

When God created the woman there was also one other consideration that God would need for his plan and it was in pregnancy for procreation. It would be necessary, if they fell, for God to create all woman with a process by which a barrier (placenta) would separate her blood from the child's blood, right from the beginning. Every human being would have his or her own DNA and blood type. He gave us a free will to make our own choices and God was prepared if they would fall because of the free will that he created in mankind. If man was to fall from grace, all children would be born of the seed of the men whose seed would then be defiled by sin and death both spiritual and later natural, and all would be born in sin.

A virgin woman would be needed to bring a male child into the world to fulfill the promise of God's plan that he had made for our redemption. The Redeemer would need to have the innocent blood for God to fulfill his promises. At the time in God's plan a virgin would be chosen to bring the Redeemer into the world. This would be an important reason why the women were to remain virgins until marriage. (*It also had to be a time in God's plan that his people were in their own land. Most conquering nations would either scattered them or take them out of their country. The chosen nation would move into the conquered nations and try to turn them all into their own; this would be the right time and place for the Redeemer to be born.*)

God's desire was for his children to be his royal family of priests that would love him and want to obey him for his eternal kingdom. This would be a long journey for all of us.

This is the simple knowledge and truth of how they fell and took all of us with them:

God created the universe and the earth for the human beings beginning with Adam and Eve. He created them so that they would know only good but still have a free will to choose to love and obey Him. God is love and his children loved Him.

The LORD planted a garden eastward in Eden and let them have dominion over the sea and over the fowl of the air, and over the cattle, and over all the earth, and over every creepy things upon the earth." Desiring to protect them, He gave Adam one command: "Of every tree in the garden you may freely eat: But of the tree of the knowledge of good and evil, you shall not eat of it: for in the day that you eat thereof thou shall surely die. A fig tree was able to put forth good figs like first ripe and, could also put forth very evil figs that cannot be eaten, they were so evil. It even had it's own wasp that without it fermenting the flowers, it would have no fruit.

God let them have an anointed cherub named Lucifer was covered with every precious stone, and had tambourines, and pipes prepared for worship, to minister with them. And in the evening God would walk with them in the garden. God had given Adam and Eve dominion over the earth, and all that he had made therein. He put them into a place of joy and peace to rule over all that he had created. God not only wanted to be their God but also a Father of them. But the beautiful shining and musical cherub, Lucifer became prideful and he arrogantly wanted to make himself like god and desired the dominion that God gave to Adam and Eve. Then he could rule it and he himself would be like God and be worshiped by man.

He used the serpent that was more cunning than any beast of the field and he chose the woman to beguile by twisting Gods words. She answered him with what Adam had told her; that they could eat of all the trees of the garden: but of the tree in the midst of the garden. God had said, "You shall not eat of the fruit of that tree nor touch it or you die." The serpent said to the woman, "You shall not surely die: for God does know that the day that you eat thereof, that your eyes will be opened, and you shall be as gods, knowing good and evil." She would be the easiest one to deceive because she had heard the command second handed but Adam was there with her. She saw that the tree was good for food, and it was pleasant to the eyes and a tree to be desired to make one wise. She took of the fruit thereof, and did eat and gave to her husband with her, and he did eat. He had led them to not believe the words that God had spoken to Adam. That they would be like gods, which was Lucifer's own desire and also became their desires. (*It is not written whether Lucifer ate from the tree while he was in the garden as a spiritual messenger prier to using the serpent to deceive Adam and Eve.*) He deceived them into desiring what he had desired and caused them to sin through unbelief and disobedience to God. Eve ate the fig from the fig tree and gave some to Adam who was there with her and their eyes were open to their nakedness. They tried to cover themselves with the large fig tree leaves but the leaves are very abrasive on one side, so it was not pleasant. When God came to the garden that evening, Adam and Eve hid. God knowing what had happened to them and what they had all done; said to Adam, "where are you?" I was afraid and naked and hid myself. God said, "Who told you that you were naked, have you eaten off the tree I commanded that you shouldn't eat? Adam said, " the woman you gave to be with me, she gave to me and I ate. God said to the woman, "what is this you have done? And the woman said, "the serpent beguiled me and I did eat. They were given one commandment and that was not to eat from the tree of the knowledge of good and evil. God said to the serpent "you shall crawl on your belly and eat dust for the rest of your life." "I will put enmity between you and the woman, and between thy seed and her seed; it shall bruise thy head and thou shall bruise his heel." Then God said to the serpent: "O Lucifer, son of the morning! How are thou fallen from heaven and cut down to the ground? You were on the holy mount of God; thou walked up and down in the midst of the stones of fire. I will cast you as profane out of the mountain of God: and I will destroy you, O covering cherub from the midst of stones of fire. Your heart is lifted up because of your beauty, and you said in your heart, I will ascend into heaven; I will exalt my throne above the stars of God. For you have also said that I will ascend above the heights of the clouds; I will be like the most high. Thou have corrupted thy wisdom by reason of thy brightness: I will cast you to the ground." God saw him as a serpent that was once his most beautiful created angel of worship music. "Yet you shall be brought down to hell. All the angels that followed you were reserved in everlasting chains under darkness unto the judgment of the great day." (This *prophecy would have to wait until its time in God's plan.)*

Adam and Eve were no longer innocents, and the Lord God said, "behold, the man is become as one of us, to know good and evil". God let Adam and Eve know what they would face in the dark world. He sent them into the harsh world to till the ground; to the man He said, "because you hearkened unto the voice of thy wife, with sweat on your face shall thou eat bread, till you return to the ground; for dust you are and to dust you shall return. To the woman He said, "I will greatly multiply thy sorrow and thy conception; in sorrow thou shall bring forth children; and your desire will be for thy husband, and he will rule over you." God exchanged their abrasive fig leaves for the skins of the innocent lamb that God had sacrificed to cover their sin of disobeying his command. There can be no redemption without the shedding of innocent blood. God had to remove them from the perfect garden, lest he put forth his hand and take and eat from "the tree of life" and all creation would remain forever in this fallen state.

What actually happened to Adam and Eve when they fell from the heavenly garden of God into the harsh world?

Firstly, the Holy Spirit no longer dwelled within them because they were no longer spiritual beings. They had the Spirit of God while they were spiritual beings in the Garden: so they would know the things that were freely given to them by God. But now they have the spirit of the world that is like a blown out candle and that has no light. They have become earthly or natural beings.

Secondly, their heart was darkened and filled with evil. The natural man receives not the things of the Spirit of God: for they are foolishness unto them: neither can they know the things of God, because they are spiritually discerned. The blood of the man became defiled because of the fall so that all children born of the seed of man would be born defiled sinners. We are not sinners because we have sinned; we are all born sinners and therefore naturally sin. God gave us a conscience so we could choose between good and evil and we still have our own free will, but with an evil nature. They continued to sacrifice innocent animals so their sins would be covered from God and they would teach their children to do the same so to cover their sins also.

Thirdly, redemption would be a longsuffering process but God so loved us that, He had made a plan to deliver us from the evil world without compromising his holiness and his divine nature. God is truth and cannot lie; neither can he fail to fulfill all his own laws, such as gravity and many more.

AFTER THE FALL:

Outside the Garden, Adam and Eve's first male child was Cain and he tilled the fields. And their second son was Abel and he kept flocks. They lived in the presence of the LORD until Cain, whose sacrifice was not with blood for the covering to the LORD but grains so God was not pleased with it and Cain became angry. God advised him and said, "If you do well, will you not be accepted? And if you do not well, sin lies at the door." But he did not listen and was angry with Abel and killed and buried his brother. God said to Cain that he was cursed from the earth and the ground would not yield a good crop and he would be a vagabond and a fugitive. Cain told the Lord that it was more than he could bear because everyone would try to kill him. God set a mark on him that who ever slayed him would have vengeance sevenfold. So he and his wife went out of the presence of the LORD and went into Nod. Adam was one hundred and thirty when he had his son in his own image and named him, Seth who would be a man of God. As time passed God had blessed Adams generations of the sons of God. Seth had Enosh and he had Cainan, and he had Mahalaleel, and he had Jared and he had Enoch and he had Methuselah and he had Lamech, and he had Noah, and he had Shem, Ham, and Japheth (triplets were quite common when the earth was being plenished.)

And it came to pass, when men began to multiply on the face of the earth, and daughters born to them were fair. The sons of God began to go out and marry the daughters of men. (*The sons of God were those that were obeying God and the other men were of the earthly generations of wicked men with Cain. Over the time frame of generations, it is believed to have grown to millions or even a few billion people on the earth.)* When the godly men's children were born from the fallen daughters, they were giants or fallen earthborn with animal and devilish minds. And God saw that the wickedness was great in the earth. And every imagination of the thoughts of their hearts was only evil continually. People became so evil that even their consciences were evil. God repented that he had made man on the earth, and it grieved him at his heart. Noah's father Lamech and grandfather Methuselah were the only family who worshiped God and they lived outside of city of Nod.

But Noah found grace in the eyes of the LORD. Noah was a just man and perfect in his generations and Noah walked with God. Noah had three sons, Shem, Ham, and Japheth. But the earth was corrupt and full of violence. Then God told Noah that the end of all flesh is come before me and I will destroy them from the earth. Make thee an ark of gopher wood and pitch inside and outside and he gave him exact dimensions. Behold I will bring a flood of waters upon the earth and destroy all flesh. But with you I will make a covenant; and you will take your family and two of every living thing, male and female and take enough food for you all. Noah did according to all God had commanded. (It has been said by some scholars that there was about a billion people on the earth at that time) Noah and his family were still the only ones who still walked with God. After about one hundred years, and the death of Lamech and then Methuselah, the four hundred and fifty foot long and seventy-five feet wide and thirty feet high ark was completed. God then told them to get all the animals and fowls into the ark and to get his family into the ark; but God left the door open for seven days of rain. We can only believe that God desired that maybe some would awaken and understand the seven days of rain and what Noah had told them about God bringing the flood was truth. No one else came except those who scorned and laughed at them. Then God closed the door. That same day all the fountains of the great deep were broken up, and the windows of heaven opened. (We can assume that other family members and friends of Noah's family now wanted them to open the door for them but it was too late to accept salvation.) And the rain was upon the earth for forty days and nights. The ark went to the top of the water, which eventually had covered the mountains. And all flesh died that moved upon the earth, both of fowl, and of cattle, and of beast, and of every creepy thing that crept on the earth and every human being. Noah only was alive and those that were with him in the ark. After one hundred and fifty days the water was gone and now God and man would start again with his plan; beginning with Noah and his wife and his three sons and their wives.

God's plan has different phases and this is the end of one and beginning of the new phase.

God is in control of His plan and we are to trust in Him until the next door is opened for our salvation. Watch and wait so you will not miss the door that is open for you.

CHAPTER 2

NOAH, BABEL, AND ABRAM

For each phase of His plan, God gives new directions:

After Noah and all that were on the ark had gone forth, he built an altar unto the Lord and took of every clean beast and fowl and offered burnt offerings on the altar. And the Lord smelled a sweet savior and said in His heart, I will not again curse the ground any more for man's sake, for the imagination of man's heart is evil from his youth; neither will I again smite any more every thing living, as I have done. While the earth remains, seedtime and harvest, and cold and heat, and summer and winter, and day and night shall not cease. And God said, This is the token of the covenant which I make between me and you and every living creature that is with you, for perpetual generations: I do set my bow in the cloud, and it shall be for a token of a covenant between me and the earth. And it shall come to pass, when I bring a cloud over the earth, that the bow shall be seen in the cloud: And I will remember my covenant, which is between me and you and every living creature of all flesh; and the waters shall no more become a flood to destroy all flesh. The fear of you and the dread of you shall be upon every beast of the earth, and upon every fowl of the air, upon all that moves upon the earth, and upon all the fishes of the sea. Into your hand they are delivered. *That is, if you can find them or catch them.* Every moving thing that lives shall be meat for you; even as the green herb have I given you all things. But the flesh with life which is the blood you may not eat the blood. Whoso sheds man's blood, by man shall his own blood be shed: for in the image of God made he man.

And the bow shall be in the cloud; and I will look upon it, that I may remember the everlasting covenant between God and every living creature of all flesh that is upon the earth.

God blessed Noah and his sons, and said to them, "Be fruitful, and multiply, and replenish the earth."

And the sons of Noah, that went forth of the ark, were Shem, and Ham, and Japheth: and Ham is the father of Canaan. Right from the beginning Noah became a husbandmen and grew a vineyard and God blessed him. He made the wine and was drunken. Ham went into his tent without an invite and saw his father was naked and then told his brothers. They took a garment on their shoulders and covered his nakedness by walking backward. When Noah awoke he knew what his younger son had done. He also knew what Shem his youngest son and Japheth his elder sons had done. He cursed Canaan, Ham's son, and said he was to be a servant of his brethren. He said, blessed be the Lord God of Shem and Canaan shall be his servant. God shall enlarge Japheth and he shall dwell in the tents of Shem and Canaan shall be his servant.

They obeyed the "be fruitful and multiply." But as time passed and the earth was being filled, God looking at his children found that they were not refilling the earth but most of the people had moved from the east to the plains of Shinar. He saw that they all together and were building a high tower to rule the earth like God. They stayed there to the fourth generation and by this time Nimrod, son of Cush, son of Ham, who began to be a mighty one in the earth. He had all the people building a city and a tower and called his kingdom Babel. All the people spoke the same language and did not want to be scattered over the earth. Nimrod wanted his tower to go up into the heavens and make a name for ourselves. But God saw what they were able to do in their wickedness with the same language and the same desire in their imaginations, there was nothing to restrain them. So the Lord said let us go down and confound their language that they may not understand one another's speech. He had to separate all of the families and did so by giving each family their own language and none could understand the other. So they went from there with only their family and obeyed God to replenish the earth. This time He scattered them all across the earth. Each family of the sons of Shem, Ham and Japheth left and began their own nations scattered abroad on the face of the earth.

Asshur, son of Shem left the land and went east and built Nineveh and the city Rehoboth and Calah and built Resen between the both, the same is a great city.

(There was about sixteen hundred years between Adam and the flood. There may have been more that a few billion people that were no more). From the flood to Babel was about one hundred seventy five years and God had been forgotten and the people worshiped idols. It began to mirror the people before the flood.

But there was one man from the family of Noah's son Shem who refused to worship wood carved gods. He began to believe that there had to be someone real and higher. Then the true living God heard him and began to show himself to him. The man's name was Abram and his wife was Sarai and God chose to build his nation through them by eventually making a covenant.

(Today we have about seven billion people on the earth and appear to be close to having more that a few billion be no more. There seems to be a great number again that have forgotten God and are worshiping things of the fallen world.)

CHAPTER 3

THE ABRAHAM COVENANT

Abram was a man from Ur of the Chaldees and lived with his father, Terah and his brother Nahor and Lot, the son of the Haran who died. Abram took a wife named Sarai and Nahor took Milcah for a wife. Terah decided to move to the land of Canaan and took Abram, Sarai and Lot with him. Terah died at two hundred and five years. The LORD spoke to Abram, who knew not this God, and he said, "Get out of your country, away from your kindred and from thy fathers house, unto a land I will show you. And I will make of thee a great nation, and I will bless you, and make thy name great; and thou shall be a blessing: And I will bless them who bless you and curse those who curse you: and in thee shall all families of the earth be blessed." So Abram departed from Haran as God had spoken unto him; and Sarai and Lot went with him along with all their substance and souls: and Abram was seventy-five years old. Abram passed into the land of Canaan and went to the place of Sichem, unto the plain of Moreh and the Canaanites were in the land. The LORD appeared unto Abram, and said, "unto thy seed will I give this land": and there he built an altar unto the LORD, who appeared unto him. He moved to the east and camped with Bethel on his west: and there built and altar unto the LORD, and called upon the name of the LORD. Then he moved south and there was a famine so he went to Egypt. He said that Sarai was his sister because they wanted her and would have killed him to keep her. They gave him many gifts for her but he and her lived. The LORD plagued Pharaoh and his house with plagues because of Sarai, Abram's wife. So they sent them and all their substance out of Egypt. He went back to Bethel very rich in cattle, silver, and in gold. Lot also was very rich and had flocks, herds, and tents and the land was not able to hold them, so they could not dwell together. Abram gave Lot the choice to the left or the right hand. Lot picked the plain that was well watered and departed. The Lord had not spoken to Abram but after Lot was separated from him, He said to Abram, "Lift up now thine eyes, and look from the place where you are to the north, and southward, and eastward, and westward: For all the land which you see, to you will I give it, and to your seed forever. And I will make your seed as the dust of the earth, then shall your seed be numbered. Arise; walk through the landing the length of it and the breath of it; for I will give unto you." Then Abram moved his tent to the plain of Mamre, which is Hebron, and built there an altar unto the LORD.

And it came to pass there was a war between four kings and five other kings and they attacked Sodom and took Lot and his family and the substance of Sodom. There was one man who escaped and told Abram the Hebrew; for he dwelt in Mamre and the Amorites that were confederates with Abram. He went and brought back all the goods, and also his brother Lot, and his goods and the women and the people. The King of Sodom went out to meet Abram and Melchizedek king of Salem brought forth bread and wine: and he was the priest of the most high God. And he blessed him, and said, "blessed be Abram of the most high God, possessor of heaven and earth: And blessed be the most high God, which hath delivered their enemies into his hand." And he gave him tithes of all. Abram said to the king of Sodom that he would not take anything from him lest he say he made Abram rich. After these things the LORD came to Abram in a vision, saying I am your shield, and thy exceeding reward. And Abram said, "LORD GOD, and what can you give me seeing I am childless?" And behold, the word of the LORD came unto him, saying, Eliezer will not be your heir; but he that shall come forth out of your bowels shall be thine heir. He brought him out and said, look to heaven, tell the number of the stars, so shall your seed be. Abram believed by faith in the hope that he would become the father of many nations, according to God's spoken word, Abram believed in the Lord and the Lord counted it to him for righteousness.

A deep sleep fell upon Abram and lo a great darkness fell upon him. God told Abram that his seed would be a stranger in a land that is not theirs, and shall serve them: and they shall afflict them four hundred years; and also that nation, whom they shall serve, will I judge: and afterward shall they come out with great substance. Thou shall go to thy fathers in peace; thou shall be buried in a good old age. But in the fourth generation they shall come hither again: for the iniquity of the Amorites is not yet full.

In that same day the Lord made a covenant with Abram, saying, Unto thy seed have I given this land, from the river of Egypt unto the great river, the river Euphrates: The Kenites, and the Kenizzites, and the Kadmonites, and the Hittites, and the Amorites, and the Canaanites, and the Girgashites, and the Jebusites.

Sarai, when she had no child for ten years, she said to Abram that the Lord had restrained her from bearing and gave her servant Hagar to Abram so Sarai could have children by her. Abram agreed and she conceived and then she despised Sarai. Things didn't go well with the situation and Abram was eighty-six years old when Ishmael was born of Hagar.

God appeared to Abram when he was ninety-nine years old and changed his name to Abraham (father of many nations) and gave an update to their covenant. God said behold, my covenant is with you and you shall be the father of many nations. I establish my covenant between me and thee and thy seed after thee in their generations for an everlasting covenant to be God unto thee, and to thy seed after thee.

(Later people will ask, "How was it then reckoned unto him for righteousness? When he was in circumcision, or in uncircumcision? It was not in circumcision, but in uncircumcision. And he received the sign of circumcision, a seal of the righteousness of the faith, which he had yet being, uncircumcised: that he might be the father of all them that believe, though they be circumcised or uncircumcised that righteousness might be imputed unto them also.)

But to the nation of Israel every man-child among you shall be circumcised. Thou shall circumcise the flesh of your foreskin and it will be a token of the covenant betwixt me and you. Those males born in your household shall at eight days be circumcised. He also changed Sarai's name to Sarah (mother of nations) and said that she would bear him a child in one year and his name will be Isaac. Abraham laughed; shall a child be born with me a hundred years old and Sarah that is ninety? Sarah had laughed also and the Lord asked, is there anything too hard for the Lord? Then Abraham circumcised all the males in his camp, including Ishmael who was thirteen years old. This was the outer showing of the covenant with God and the nation of Israel.

Sarah was with child at the time the Lord had said and she gave birth to Isaac. When Isaac was eight days old Abraham circumcised him and when he weaned, Abraham made a great feast for him and Ishmael was mocking Isaac. Sarah told Abraham to send him and the Egyptian away. The thing was very grievous in Abraham's sight because of Ishmael, his son. God told him not to grieve over the lad that he would make Ishmael a nation because he is thy seed. In all that Sarah has said to thee, hearken unto her voice; for in Isaac shall thy seed be called. Abraham obeyed and sent her and the child away. Abraham sojourned in the Philistines land many days.

God told Abraham, take now thy son, your only son Isaac, whom thou loves, and get thee into the land of Moriah; and offer him there for a burnt offering upon one of the mountains, which I will tell you of. And Abraham rose up early in the morning and saddled his ass, and took two of his young men with him, Isaac his son, and some split wood for the burnt offering, went to the place of which God had told him. Then on the third day Abraham lifted his eyes and saw the place far off. Abraham told the young men to stay and that he and his son will go yonder and worship, and come again to you. Abraham placed the wood and laid it upon Isaac his son; and he took the fire and the knife; and both went together. Isaac said to Abraham his father: Behold the fire and the wood; but where is the lamb for the burnt offering? Abraham said, my son God will provide himself a lamb for the burnt offering. And they came to the place where God had told them of; and Abraham built an altar there and laid the wood in order. He then bound Isaac his son and the son trusted in his father and he laid him on the altar onto the wood. Abraham, trusting in his God, stretched forth his hand and took the knife to slay his son. But the angel of the LORD called out to him from heaven, and said, Abraham, Abraham: and he answered, Here am I. And the angel said, do not lay a hand upon the lad, neither do thou any thing to him: for now I know that thou fears God, seeing thou has not withheld thy son, thine only son from Me.

(This is a picture of what would come when God so loved the world that He will give his only begotten Son and the Son will give his life in love so we sinners may live in him. The Christ comes into the world to die and save all sinners of the world.)

Abraham lifted up his eyes and saw a ram caught in the thicket by his horns: he took it and used him for the burnt offering instead of his son. A second time the angel called out to him, and said, By myself have I sworn, said the LORD, for because thou has done this thing, and has not withheld thy son, your thine only son: That in blessing I will bless thee, and in multiplying I will multiply thy seed as stars of the heaven, and as the sand which is on the seashore; and thy seed shall possess the gate of his enemies; and thy seed shall all the nations of the earth be blessed; because thou has obeyed my voice.

As it came to pass, Nahor, Abraham's brother had many children and Isaac was thirty-six when his mother Sarah died, and Isaac missed her. Abraham sent his servant to his brother's family to get a wife for Isaac. The servant prayed to the Lord to bring the woman he wanted for Isaac and he brought Rebekah to him and he brought her to Isaac. She became his wife and he loved her and was comforted after his mother's death. Then Isaac prayed for his wife to have children and she was having a hard pregnancy and inquired of the Lord as to why. The Lord told her that she had two nations and two manner of people, one stronger than the other people and the elder will serve the younger. Isaac had twin boys by Rebekah, Esau that was covered with red hair and Jacob, who took hold of Esau's heel. Esau grew and became a cunning hunter and Isaac loved him because he did eat of his venison. Jacob was a plain man, dwelling in tents and made boiled pottage but Rebekah loved him. Esau came in from hunting and said to Jacob, give me some of your red stew for I am faint. Jacob said, this day sell me your birthright. Esau said, what good is a birthright if I am at the point of death. So Esau agreed and sold him his birthright as the firstborn. When Isaac was very old, he told Esau to go get some game and make him some stew and he would pass the blessing down to him. Rebekah heard him and set up a way to deceive Isaac to bless Jacob instead. Esau had already traded his birth right for some stew. Now Jacob would get his blessing too. The Lord had told Rebekah that the elder would serve the younger and it came to be true through her deception.

Rebekah dressed up Jacob to feel and smell like Esau being Isaac could not see any more. "The blessing" that Isaac was to give Esau was given to Jacob and both were very upset. Esau was going to wait till Isaac died and then kill Jacob and get them both back. Rebekah heard and went to Isaac and asked him to send Jacob to her brother's house to get a wife. Isaac and his wife were at grief when Esau married the Hittite women. Isaac blessed Jacob and he left. His mother would not see her beloved son again.

Jacob was blessed by God to give birth to His Nation of Israel.

Jacob and the Beginning of a Nation

Jacob set out on his journey toward Haran and when the sun was set he piled stones for a pillow and lay down to sleep. He dreamed that there was a ladder set upon the earth and the top of it reached into heaven and angels of God ascending and descending on it. Then he saw the Lord stood above it and He renewed the covenant with Jacob. The Lord said, "I am the Lord God of Abraham thy father and the God of Isaac: the land where you lie, to you I will give it and your seed; and your seed shall be as the dust of the earth, and you shall spread abroad to the west, and to the east, and to the north, and to the south: and in you and your seed shall all the families of the earth be blessed. And, behold, I am with you and will keep you wherever you go, and will bring you again into this land; for I will not leave you until I have done that which I have spoken to you of." Jacob awoke and said, surely the Lord is in this place; and I knew it not. How dreadful is this place! This is none other but the house of God, and this is the gate to heaven. He took the stone that was his pillow and made a pillar and poured oil over it and called the name of the place Beth-el made a vow to God. "If God will be with me, and will keep me in this way that I go, and will give me bread to eat, and raiment to put on, so that I come again to my father's house in peace; then shall the Lord be my God: and this stone which I have set for a pillar, shall be God's house: and of all you shall give me I will surely give the tenth unto you."

Jacob came upon a well in Haran and asked the men with the sheep if they knew Laban. They said yes and pointed out Rachel his daughter. Jacob saw Rachel and went and removed the stone and watered the sheep. And Jacob kissed Rachel and told her whom he was and wept, and she ran to tell her father. Jacob said he would serve Laban for seven years for Rachel to be his wife for he loved her dearly. When it was time it seemed but a few days to Jacob for the love he had for her. He went to Laban and asked for his wife. Laban gathered all the men together for a great feast and in the evening, he brought Leah, his elder daughter instead of Rachel and Jacob went in to her. Come morning Jacob saw that it was Leah and accused Laban of beguiling him. Laban said: in his country the youngest could not be married before the eldest, but after Leah fulfilled her week and you agree to serve for seven more years; Rachel can be your wife also. Jacob agreed and did so. *(It is not hard to see that deceit and beguiling was familiar to this family.)*

Jacob did not love Leah but she blessed him with children. She bore four sons, Reuben, Simeon, Levi, and Judah. But after Ruben she said, God saw her affliction and now Jacob would love her, and after Simeon, she said because she was hated the Lord gave her this son. After Levi she said now this time my husband will be joined to me. Then after Judah she said, now I will praise the Lord and left bearing. She had thought she could take Jacob away from Rachel because she gave no children to Jacob. Then Rachel began to envy her sister and gave her maid Bilhah to Jacob to have children for her. Bilhah bore Dan, Naphtali for Rachel and she had prevailed over Leah. Then Leah gave her maid to Jacob and Zilpah bare Gad and Asher. Then Leah bore Issachar, Zebulun and daughter Dinah. After she had Zebulun she said, God has endued me a good dowry; now my husband will dwell with me because I have given him six sons. God remembered Rachel and opened her womb and she conceived and bore a son Joseph and said," the Lord shall add to me another son." Then Jacob said for Laban to send him away to his own place and country. "Since I have been with you the Lord has blessed and greatly multiplied your cattle." Laban did not see it that way so they made a deal for dividing any new cattle. Jacob would get all the weak cattle but the Lord showed Jacob what he needed to do to get what the Lord wanted him to have. The angel of God had come to help Jacob. The angel of God spoke to Jacob in a dream and said," look up and see, all the rams that leap upon the cattle are ring staked, speckled and grisled and Jacob obeyed and received a huge strong herd. Jacob told his wives that, even though Laban did not have good continence to him and God suffered him not to hurt me: for I have seen all that Laban did to you. "I am the God of Bethel where you anointed the pillar, and vowed the vow unto me: now rise and get out of this land." The Lord said to Jacob, " return to the land of thy father and to thy kindred and I will be with you." Jacob rose up and set his wives and children onto camels and all that was his that he had gotten in Padanaram and left while Laban was shearing his sheep in the mountains.

When Jacob was on route to his father, Laban caught up to him in Mount Gilead. Jacob told him that it had been twenty years in his house, I served fourteen years for your two daughters, and six years for your cattle and you change my wages ten times. Except the God of my father, the God of Abraham, and the fear of Isaac, had been with me, surely you would have sent me now empty. God has seen my affliction and the labor of my hands, and rebuked you yester-night. Then Jacob built a pillar with a vow that would be a witness between them and God would watch that they do not pass over for harm. Jacob called the pillar, Galeed and they both parted in the morning.

The angels of God met Jacob on his way and when he saw them, he said, this is God's host: and he called the place Mahanaim (two camps). And Jacob sent messengers before him to Esau his brother unto the land of Seir, the country of Edom. They were to tell him that: thy servant Jacob says thus, I have sojourned with Laban and stayed there till now: and I have oxen, and asses, flocks, and menservants, and women servants: and I have sent to tell my lord, that I may find grace in thy sight. They returned and said that Esau was coming to meet him with four hundred men. Jacob sent messengers to Esau that he was coming to him with gifts. And would line them in three different droves.

He then went alone to pray before the Lord and ask for deliverance for all of them from Esau. And he reminded the Lord of his promise at Bethel. He sent many sheep and goats to Esau from his servant, Jacob in three droves before he would see him and send them across. Then Jacob rose up that night and took his two wives and his two women servants and his eleven sons to the other side of the fork of Jabbok River.

It was the last night when he was alone and there wrestled with a man until the breaking of day. When he saw that he was not winning, the man touched the hollow of Jacob's thigh and put it out of joint. The man said, let me go, for the day is breaking. He held onto the man and said I will not let you go until you bless me. The man said his name would no longer be Jacob but "*Israel*": for as a prince have you power with God and with men, and hast prevailed. And he blessed him. Jacob called that place Peniel, for I have seen God face to face and my life is preserved. He named the place, Peniel.

Jacob lifted up his head and saw Esau was there. He passed over the river and divided the children between his wives and women servants and put them behind him and bowed himself before Esau seven times. But Esau was humbled and they came together and wept. Esau then went back to Seir and Jacob stopped at Succoth and then moved into the land of Canaan at Shalem, a city of Shechen. He bought a parcel of a field, where he spread his tent, at the hand of the children of Hamor, Shechem's father, for a hundred pieces of money. He erected there an altar, and called it El-elohe-Israel. But problems arose between them so God sent them to Bethel where he had built an altar to God when he had fled Esau. Jacob called for all the false gods to be given to him and they all gave them to Jacob and he buried them under an oak tree by Shechem. They went to Bethel and remember all the Lord had said to him. God renewed his covenant and his name, Israel. They journeyed then to Ephrath.

When they were a little way outside of Ephrath, Rachel had hard labor and delivered a boy child and she called him Benoni but Jacob called him Benjamin and Rachel died and was buried in the way of Bethlehem. Jacob set a pillar upon her grave. He then went out Mamre in Hebron where Isaac and Abraham sojourned. Isaac died after one hundred eighty years. Esau and Jacob buried him.

Now the sons of Jacob (Israel) were twelve: of Leah; Reuben, Simeon, Levi, Judah, Issachar and Zebulun; of Rachel; Joseph and Benjamin; of Bilhah, Rachel's handmaid; Dan and Naphtali: and of Zilpah, Leah's handmaid; Gad and Asher.

These would become the twelve tribes of Israel, and the first part of God's promise to Abraham and Jacob. God told Jacob in Bethel "In thee and thy seed shall all the families of the earth be blessed." They would be the beginning of the nation of Israel that would bring the anointed one to complete the covenant.

CHAPTER 4

ISRAEL'S JOURNEY
TO EGYPT

Israel's sons were jealous because he loved Joseph more than all his children. He was the son of Rachel, the woman he loved. Joseph also kept seeing in dreams; all his brothers bowing down to him. Joseph was seventeen when Jacob made him a coat of many colors and his brothers envied him. He then sent Joseph to check on his ten brothers who were watching the sheep. The brothers grew angry when they saw him in his fancy coat and his telling them what to do. They talked of killing him, but Reuben said, shed no blood, just put him down the dry well, for he planned to rescue him later. Judah looked up and said unto his brothers, what profit is it if we slay our brother, and conceal his blood? There were some Ishmeelites passing by on the way to Egypt, Judah said let us sell him; we wont have to put our hand on him. So they sold him for twenty pieces of silver and the Ishmeelites took him as a slave to Egypt. Reuben returned to get the boy and he was not in the pit. They had taken his coat and covered it with kid of goat's blood and then said a wild animal must have gotten him. When they told their father, Jacob, he could not be comforted from the loss of his favorite son, especially since his wife had waited so long to give him a child.

This is where people begin to ask, "Where was God, why did He allow that to happen to Joseph?" These are the same questions we ask today. But God provided us with an explanation. This evil thing was done by the will of the nine brothers; because of their disobedience to God's will. We need to understand in our lives; that bad things can happen to good people and we can see that it was not only the brothers were doing evil but so was Joseph. He strutted about and was very prideful and harassed them because his father loved him more than them. His ways are not the same as ours but He does always provide an escape from the trouble we get ourselves into. We can see the change both in the brothers and in Joseph but it is too late to go back. The brothers felt the guilt and remorse because of how it hurt their father. Joseph came to himself when he was humbled as a slave but he repented and continued to believe that God was with him and would take care of him. This is a picture of that which the Messiah endured when he came to earth but he did not retaliate. This picture is also given to us so that we all could be like Joseph and when bad times come our way, we can keep our faith in God. His plan covers so much time and so many people that it is difficult for us to fathom the vast greatness of our God.

Joseph reached Egypt and was bought as a slave by Potipher, an officer of the Pharaoh.

The Lord was with Joseph and he was a prosperous man. His master saw the Lord was with him and that the Lord made all that he did to prosper in his hands. Joseph found grace in his sight and he made him the overseer of his house. God blessed the Egyptian's house for Joseph's sake. Joseph was a goodly person, and well favored. The master's wife cast her eyes upon Joseph and said, "lie with me." But he refused and said to her, "Behold, there is none greater in this house than I, neither has he kept anything from me except his wife. How can I do this great wickedness and sin against God?" This went on day after day and he listened not to her. One day he came into the house to do business and no men were there; she grabbed by his garment and said, "lie with me." He left his garment in her hand and fled. She then called the men of the house and accused him of coming in to lie with her and she cried out in aloud voice. Then he left his garment and fled. The husband believed and was angered and sent him to the prison where the king's prisoners were bound. But the Lord was with Joseph and showed him mercy, and gave him favor in the sight of the keeper of the prison. He made him to be over all the prisoners and he could see that the Lord was with him because anything that was under his hand, The Lord made it prosper. And it came to pass that the butler and the baker offended their lord the king of Egypt and he put them into the prison where Joseph was bound. After a season they each had a dream in the same night and each according to their position. They told Joseph that they had both had a dream but no interpreter. Joseph said to them, do not all interpretations belong to God? Tell me them, I pray you.

They did and Joseph told the butler in three days the king restore him to his place. Joseph asked him to remember him to the Pharaoh that he had done nothing wrong. When the baker saw that it was good wanted his interpreted and Joseph told him that in three days he would be hung. In three days the butler was restored and the baker was hung. It was two years and the butler said nothing to the Pharaoh. Then the Pharaoh had a dream and woke up, and then he had a second dream. He called all his magicians of Egypt and told them of his dreams but none could interpret them. The butler then spoke up about Joseph interpreting both his dream and the baker's demise. Joseph was thirty years old *when the* Pharaoh sent for Joseph and they gave him raiment to go before him; I understand that you interpret dreams. Joseph said it is not in me: God will give Pharaoh an answer of peace. Pharaoh told him both dreams and Joseph told him that it was one. God has shown Pharaoh what he is about to do. The seven good cows are seven years; and the seven good ears are seven years: the dream is one. And the seven thin and ill-favored cows that came up after them are seven years and the seven empty ears blasted with the east wind shall be seven years of famine. Behold, there is seven years of great plenty throughout Egypt: and there shall arise after seven years of famine; and all the plenty will be forgotten in the land of Egypt and the famine will consume the land. Now therefore let Pharaoh seek a man that is discreet and wise, and set him over the land of Egypt. Let Pharaoh do this, and let him appoint officers over the land, and take up the fifth part of the land of Egypt in the seven plenteous years. Let them gather all the food of those good years, and lay up corn under the hand of Pharaoh, and let them keep food in the cities. And that food shall be for the store to the land against the seven years of famine, which shall be in the land of Egypt; that the land perish not through the famine. The thing was good in the eyes of Pharaoh and the eyes of his servants. Pharaoh said unto Joseph, forasmuch as God has shown you all this, there is none as discreet and wise as you are. Thou shall be over my house, and according unto thy word shall all my people be ruled: only in the throne will I be greater than you.

See I set you over all the land of Egypt and he put his ring upon Joseph's finger. He changed Joseph's name to Zaphnathpaaneah and gave him to wife Asenath the daughter of Potipherah priest of On. Asenath bore him two sons, Manasseh and Ephraim in Egypt.

The seven years of plenteous went and the famine was over all the earth; and Joseph opened all the storehouses and sold to the Egyptians. And all countries came unto Egypt to Joseph to buy corn because the famine was so severe in all lands.

Jacob saw that there was corn in Egypt and sent his sons, except for Benjamin, to buy corn. When they reached Egypt

Joseph recognized them but they did not recognize him. He called them spies but they denied it and told of all his family including Joseph's brother, Benjamin and their father. He spoke to the brothers through an interpreter and listened to them as they spoke to one another about Joseph. They were talking about their guilt in that they had seen the anguish of his soul, when he besought us, and we would not hear, therefore this distress has come upon us. Reuben answered them, spoke I not unto you saying do not sin against the child and you would not hear? Therefore behold, also his blood is required.

They began again to be guilty of the evil thing they had done because now they found the money they paid for the food was in one of the bags of corn. They cried out and said, "What is this that God has done to us?" And their heart failed them because they knew they would have to go back with Benjamin in order to get Simeon back. Convincing his father, Israel to trust them to take Benjamin was not easy because his brother Joseph was dead and his father could not be comforted. He would die if anything happened to Benjamin. Reuben finally convinced him because he promised him that he could slay his two sons if he didn't bring him back. Israel said, "God almighty give you mercy before the man that he may send away your other brother and Benjamin. If I bereaved of my children, I am bereaved."

When they reached Egypt, Joseph saw Benjamin and said to the ruler of his house for them to be brought to his house and have lunch made ready. The men were all afraid because they were at the house and of the money left in their sacks. They spoke to the steward about the sacks and they didn't know who put them in the sacks. The steward said, "Peace be to you, fear not: your God, and the God of your father, hath given you treasure in your sacks." They sat for lunch and spent the night. Joseph told his steward to fill their sacks with corn and the money and put his silver cup in the sack of the youngest. They left early in the morning and they had gotten out of the city not far; Joseph sent his steward to say to them, wherefore have you rewarded evil for good? The brothers said they would not do such a thing and that they could kill the one whom stole it and we also will be my lord's bondmen. The steward said, "let it be according to your words." The cup was found in Benjamin's sack and they tore their clothes and laded every man his ass and returned to the city. Judah and his brethren came to Josephs house and fell before him on the ground. And Joseph said, what deed is this that you have done? Think you not that such a man as I can certainly divine? And Judah said, "what shall we say unto the lord? What shall we speak?" God has found out the iniquity of thy servants: behold, we are and he also with whom the cup is found. An Joseph said, God forbid that I should do so: but the man in whose hand the cup is found, he shall be my servant; and as for you, get you up in peace to your father. Judah spoke of his father, an old man, and a child of hid old age, a little one; his brother is dead, and he alone is left of his mother, and his father loves him. The lad cannot leave his father or his father would die. Now therefore I pray thee, let thy servant abide instead of the lad a bondman to my lord; and let the lad go with his brethren. For how shall I go up to my father, and the lad be not with me? If peradventure, I see the evil that shall come on my father. Joseph could not refrain himself and told all the Egyptians to leave. And Joseph said to his brethren, "I am Joseph your brother, whom you sold into Egypt." And he wept aloud and the brethren drew near and wept. Now therefore do not be grieved, or angry with yourselves that you sold me hither: God did send me before you to preserve life. For two years there has been famine in the land: and yet there are five more in which we cannot harvest. God sent me before you to preserve you a posterity in the earth, and to save your lives. So now it as not you that sent me but God: and he made me a father to Pharaoh, and lord of his house, and a rule throughout the land of Egypt. Haste you to my father and say to him, thus says your son Joseph, God has made me lord of all Egypt: come down to me, tarry not; and thou shall live in Goshen, and thou shall be near to me. He fell upon his brother Benjamin's neck and wept and Benjamin wept upon his neck. Israel took his journey with all he had and came to Beer-sheba and offered sacrifices to God of his father Isaac. For God spoke unto Israel in the visions of the night, and said, Jacob, Jacob, Fear not to go down to Egypt; for I will there make of you a great nation: I will go down with you into Egypt; and I will surely bring you up again; and Joseph shall put his hand upon your eyes. And Jacob rose up and continued to Egypt. All the souls that came with Jacob into Egypt, which came out of his loins, besides Jacobs sons' wives were sixty-six; Josephs wife and two sons that were born in Egypt brought the nation to seventy souls. When they came, Judah went ahead to Joseph for directions to Goshen and brought them into Goshen. Joseph readied his chariot and went up to Goshen to meet his father, Israel. He fell on his neck and wept on his neck for a good while. And Israel said to Joseph, now let me die, since I have seen your face, because you are yet alive.

Jacob lived seventeen years in Egypt and blessed all his sons and Josephs sons. But he had blessed Ephraim, the youngest, with his right hand and Manasseh with the left; Joseph tried to change it but Jacob refused. He said that he also shall become a people and shall be great: but the younger shall be greater than he, and his seed shall become a multitude of nations. Israel said unto Joseph, Behold I die: but God shall be with you, and bring you again unto the land of your fathers. Moreover I have given to you one portion above your brethren, which I took out of the hand of the Amorite with my sword and with my bow. Israel (Jacob) died at the age of one hundred forty seven and Joseph had the physicians embalm him. They journeyed to the cave in the field of Machpelah, which is before Mamre, in the land of Canaan, which Abraham had bought for a buryingplace. There they had buried Abraham, Sarah, Isaac, Rebekeh, and Leah, and now buried Israel in the tomb that Abraham had purchased. Joseph returned to Egypt and reassured his brothers that God did it all for their good. He lived another fifty-four years and saw the children of Ephraim's third generation: and also of Machir the son of Manasseh, and blessed them. Joseph said to his brethren, I die: and God will surely visit you, and bring you out of this land unto the land which he swear to Abraham, to Isaac, and to Jacob. He took an oath to the children of Israel, saying God will surely visit you and you will carry my bones from Egypt. Joseph died at the age of one hundred and ten years old and they embalmed him and he was put in a coffin in Egypt. The number of the Hebrews had grown to mighty numbers and a new Pharaoh of Egypt, that did not know Joseph, and feared the number of them growing.

The Egyptians made the children of Israel serve them with rigor. The Pharaoh tried to kill all newborn males of the Hebrews through the midwives but they feared God. Then he told the soldiers to throw them in the river.

One child, Moses was hidden and survived.

God fulfilled all of the promises and prophecies that Abram was foretold and the great substance for the nation of Israel. It is as written in Gen 15:13-14, "Israel had been in Egypt the four hundred years." (But the best was yet to come).

CHAPTER 5

MOSES AND EGYPT REDEMPTION

A Levite couple, Amram and Jochebed had a male child that they said was a goodly child so they hid him for three months. When she could not hide him any longer she took for him an ark of bulrushes, and daubed it with slime and with pitch, and put the child therein; and she laid it in the flags by the river's brink. His sister went along out of sight to watch him. The daughter of Pharaoh was bathing and her maidens walked along the riverside when she saw the ark among the flags and told her maiden to go get it. When she opened and saw the child; and behold the babe wept. And she had compassion on him and said this is one of the Hebrew's children. Then his sister said to Pharaoh's daughter, should I go get a nurse of the Hebrew women that she might nurse the child for you? She said, go and the maid went and called the child's mother. And Pharaoh's daughter said to her, take the child, Moses away, and nurse him for me, and I will give you your wages. She called him Moses because she drew him out of the water. And the woman took the child and nursed it. And the child grew and was brought to Pharaoh's daughter and he became her son and called him Moses. He was learned in all the wisdom of the Egyptians, and was mighty in words and deeds.

And it came to pass in those days, when Moses was fully grown at forty years old; that he began to look upon the burdens of his brethren, the Hebrews. He came upon an Egyptian smiting a Hebrew; he looked this way and that way, and when there was no man, he slew the Egyptian and buried him in the sand. When he went out on the second day, two men of the Hebrews strove together: and he said to them that did wrong, why do you smite thy fellow? Who made you a prince and a judge over us? You intend to kill me, as you killed the Egyptian? And Moses feared and said, surely this thing is known. Now when Pharaoh heard this thing, he sought to slay Moses. (When Stephen spoke before the council, he said that Moses smote the Egyptian, the Hebrews refused him; for he supposed his brethren would have understood how that God by his hand would deliver them, but they understood not.)

But Moses had fled to Midian: and set down at a well. The priest of Median, Jethro had seven daughters and they came to water their flock but the shepherds drove them away: but Moses helped them and watered their sheep. The women went home and told their father, Reul (Jethro) that an Egyptian had delivered them from the shepherds. Moses came and was content to stay with Jethro and he gave Moses his daughter, Zipporah to be his wife. She gave him a son and named him Gershom. And it came to pass that the king of Egypt died and the children of Israel cried out to God by reason of bondage.

Moses kept the flock of Jethro, his father-in-law for forty years and he as he led the flock to the backside of desert came to the mountain of God, even Horeb. An angel of the Lord appeared to him in a flame of fire out of the midst of a bush: and he looked, and behold, bush burned with fire, but the bush was not consumed. He went to see why the bush was not burnt. And when the Lord saw that he turned aside to see, God called unto him out of the midst of the bush, and said, Moses, Moses. And he said here am I.

Come no closer, take off your shoes for the place where you stand is holy ground. I am the God of your father, the God of Abraham, the God of Isaac, and the God of Jacob.

And Moses hid his face; for he was afraid to look upon God. And the Lord said, I have surely seen the affliction of my people which are in Egypt, and have heard their cry by reason of their taskmasters; for I know their sorrows; and I am come down to deliver them out of the hand of the Egyptians, and to bring them up out of the land unto a good land and a large, unto a land flowing with milk and honey; unto the place of the Canaanites, and the Hittites, and the Amorites, and the Perizzites, and the Hivites and the Jebusites. Now therefore, behold the cry of the children of Israel is come to me: and I have seen the oppression wherewith the Egyptians oppress them.

Come now therefore, and I will send you to Pharaoh, that you may bring forth my children of Israel out of Egypt. Moses said to God, Who am I, that I should go unto Pharaoh, and that I should bring forth the children of Israel out of Egypt? (After forty years, had Moses forgotten that God by his hand delivered him? Was it because of his own timing, when thought he could deliver them himself when he was younger? Or was it because in Gods timing that he would be called to deliver those who rejected him at the age of eighty. Is that why he doubted?) And God said, certainly I will be with you. Moses asked, who do I say that you are when I approach the children of Israel? And God said, I AM that I AM have sent you: and when you have brought forth the people out of Egypt, you shall serve God upon this mountain, Mt. Horab. Tell them exactly what I said, that God said that I AM that I AM: and he said, thus shall you say unto the children of Israel, I AM has sent me to you. Go and gather the elders of Israel and say to them, The Lord God of your fathers, the God of Abraham, the God of Isaac, the God of Jacob has appeared unto me and sent me unto you to say, I have surely visited you, and seen that which is done to you in Egypt: And I will bring you out of the affliction of Egypt. They will hearken unto your voice: and you and the elders will go before the king of Egypt, and you shall say to him, "the Lord of the Hebrews has met with us: now let us go, we beseech thee, three days' journey into the wilderness, that we may sacrifice to the Lord our God." And I am sure that the king of Egypt will not let you go, no, not by a mighty hand. And I will stretch out my hand and smite Egypt with all my wonders, which I will do in the midst thereof: and after that he will let you go. I will give this people favor in the sight of the Egyptians and you will not go empty but you will spoil the Egyptians.

God told him of signs but he had doubts that they would believe him. The LORD said, what is that in your hand? And he said a rod. God said, cast it on the ground, and it became a serpent and Moses fled from it. And the LORD told him to put forth his hand and take it by the tail. He did it and it became a rod in his hand: that they may believe that the LORD God of their fathers, the God of Abraham, the God of Isaac, and the God of Jacob has appeared to you. Then he told him to put his hand into your bosom and he took it out and it was leprous as snow. He then said put your hand unto your bosom and bring it out and it turned again as his flesh. Then he gave him another wonder; take some water out of the river and when you pour it on dry land it will turn into blood. Then Moses said, O my LORD, I am slow in speech and slow of tongue.

God answered him, who has made your mouth? Or who makes the dumb, or blind or deaf? Have not I the LORD? Now therefore go, and I will be with your mouth and teach you what to say. Moses wanted him to send someone else and the anger of the LORD was kindled against Moses. He said to him, is not Aaron the Levite your brother? I know he can speak well. And also behold, he is coming to meet you and when he sees you, he will be glad in his heart. You will tell Aaron all that I say to you and he will speak for you. They came together and Aaron and Moses with Zipporah his wife and Gershom and Eliezer his sons left for Egypt.

The covenant made with Abraham, Isaac, and Jacob and Joseph in Egypt gave the importance of the circumcision. God said, to Abraham, My covenant shall be in your flesh for an everlasting covenant. And uncircumcised man-child whose flesh of his foreskin is not circumcised, that soul shall be cut off from his people; he has broken my covenant. Moses was guilty of not circumcising his firstborn son. He, his wife and sons stopped at an Inn; when God sent his Angel to kill his first son, Gershom. Zipporah recognized what the Lord had said for Moses to tell the Pharaoh was also for her firstborn son, and he was in danger. She took a stone knife and circumcised her son and threw it at Moses and said, a bloody husband you are to me. So he let him go: then she said, a bloody husband you are because of the circumcsion. The Lord said that his son would not have been able to serve him if not under the covenant. Moses then sent Zipporah and the children back to Jethro. Aaron and Moses left for Egypt and did all that God had asked of them. They first brought the elders to believe that God had visited them and then went to Pharaoh to ask to go out three days' journey to worship their God and the Pharaoh refused and said no more straw to make bricks will be given to you, get your own but with the same quota.

There were 10 plagues God sent to Egypt to show the world that He is the one true God and in his power He put to shame 9 of their gods. These plagues occurred within a period of nine months: (KJV)

1. The water of the Nile River turned to blood (Ex 7:14-25)

2. Frogs overran the river into houses (Ex 8:1-15)

3. People and animals infested with lice. All the dust became lice (Ex 8: 16-19)

4. Swarms of flies cover the land except Goshen (Ex 8: 20-32)

5. Disease killed all Egypt's livestock (Ex 9: 1-7)

6. Ashes brought boils infecting Egyptians and animals (Ex 9: 8-12)

7. Hail and fire destroyed the fields and all in the fields (Ex 9:13-35)

8. Locusts covered all the land and ate what was left from the hail (Ex 10:1-20)

9. Thick darkness cover Egypt for three days except the Hebrews (Ex 10: 21-29)

10. Egyptians first born, people and animals, were destroyed by God's death angel (Ex 11:1-12:30)

God gave the Hebrews instructions so that their firstborns will be saved and it would be done as a memorial after completed in Egypt. Instructions for now and future: This month will be the first month of the year to you. In the tenth day of the month every man of house will choose a lamb or goat without blemish, a male of the first year and take it out of the herd and keep it until the fourteenth day. The whole congregation will kill the animal in the evening and put the blood on the two sides of the doorposts and across the upper doorpost. Eat the flesh that night with unleavened bread and bitter herbs. Roasted and any leftovers burned before morning. Be dressed and ready to go in the night.

I will pass over you at midnight and the plague shall not be upon you to destroy you, when I smite the land of Egypt. This day will be unto you a memorial and you will keep it a Memorial unto the Lord throughout your generations, you shall keep it a Memorial by an ordinance forever.

When the Pharaoh's son died, he and the Egyptians were urgent to get them all out of Egypt and they all left after *four hundred and thirty years* and took Joseph's remains with them. God led them toward the Red Sea, but he also hardened the heart of Pharaoh who pursued after the children of Israel. Pharaoh took six hundred chosen chariots and all the chariots of Egypt and captains over each one of them. The children of Israel saw them and cried out to the LORD. Moses told the people not to fear, stand still and see the salvation of the Lord, he will show you today: for the Egyptians whom you have seen today, you shall see them no more. The Lord will fight for you, and you will hold your peace. And the LORD said to Moses, wherefore cry thou unto me? Speak to the children of Israel, that they go forward: But lift your rod, and stretch out your hand over the sea and divide it: and the children of Israel shall go on dry ground through the midst of the sea. The Egyptians shall know that I am the LORD, when I have gotten me honor upon Pharaoh, upon his chariots, and upon his horsemen.

The angel of the LORD moved the cloud from before them and put it between them and the Egyptians. They could not see each other. It was light on the Hebrews but dark on the Egyptians all night. The Lord told Moses to stretch out his hand over the sea; and caused the sea to go back by a strong east wind all that night, and made the sea dry ground; and the children of Israel went into the midst of the sea on dry ground and the waters were a wall unto them on their right hand, and on their left. It came to pass, that in the morning watch, the Egyptians pursued them on dry ground but when in the midst of the sea the wheels of the chariots began to sink in mud. They took off the wheels and said, let us flee from the face of Israel: for the LORD fights for them against the Egyptians. The Lord told Moses to stretch his hand over the sea and the sea returned to his strength and the LORD overthrew the Egyptians in the midst of the sea.

Thus the LORD *saved Israel that day out of the hand of the Egyptians and Israel saw the Egyptians dead on the seashore.*

And Israel saw that great work which the LORD did upon the Egyptians: and the people feared the LORD and believed the LORD, and his servant Moses.

Moses and the children of Israel sang a song to the LORD;

I will sing to the LORD, for he has triumphed gloriously: the horse and the rider has he thrown into the sea. The Lord is my strength and song, and he has become my salvation: He is my God, and I will prepare a habitation; my father's God, and I will exalt him. The LORD is a man of war: the LORD is his name... Who is like unto thee, O LORD, among the gods? Who is like thee, glorious in holiness, fearful in praises, doing wonders? Thou in thy mercy have led forth a people, which thou have redeemed: thou have guided them in thy strength unto thy holy habitation.... The LORD shall reign forever and ever.

God used signs and wonders to destroy the Egyptians and free his people. The wonders that God had done spread all over the world and they all knew that God was the most high God and extremely powerful and most feared him. His own people began to fear him and believe that he is the Great God of Israel. I believe that God's heart was very full of love for his people at this wonderful moment in time.

Looking at the big picture from God's view of the beginning of his plan for all of his children to eventually be ready for the Kingdom of his Son. This picture of God's longsuffering for the four hundred and thirty years to pass; and waiting for the time generations of the nation of Israel would all call out to him to bring them out of bondage. To think that the Lord had brought the Egyptians to their knees with ten supernatural events in about 60 days and brought them out of Egypt for the greatest event of all. The holding back the Red Sea for hundreds of thousands of people to cross on dry land. God had already told Abraham that this bondage would happen to his seed and how long they would be in Egypt and when he would bring them out of bondage. But by this time Moses when he returned to Egypt even the story of what God did through Joseph's life had long been forgotten. How God saved them all through the famine of seven years; and kept them in peace while Joseph and the Pharaoh lived. Many had abandoned it all and after many generations they adapted to the ways of Egypt. The elders went through the motions about God but appeared to be in unbelief and had lost hope. When the afflictions had become unbearable, they began to cry out to God and he heard them.

There were about 70 males that went into Egypt and about 603,550 that came out of Egypt old enough to go forth to war Moses sang his song with the mission that the LORD had laid out for them to take the holy habitation of the LORD in Zion. All the inhabitants of the land of Canaan shall melt away.

This is pretty much where we are today. God has been forgotten from generation to generation from the lack of teaching the Gospel of Paul that he received directly from the Lord Jesus Christ. By grace through faith we can walk in the way of God; but we are becoming more and more adapted to the ways of the world. But we can still cry out to God and he will hear us if we believe that he is who he says he is and does what he says he will do. He truly loves us all and will bring all those who believe on the planet back under the authority of God.

It always seems that heaven on earth is just over the next hill but there is still a long way to go in God's plan. And we will continue all through time to have great hope for the final completion of his marvelous plan when we can all be with him forever.

CHAPTER 6

WILDERNESS EXPERIENCE

All the Hebrew people were singing and believed that the power of the God of Israel delivered them from slavery in Egypt. They went into Egypt with seventy men and came out with six hundred and three thousand five hundred fifty men able to go to war.

The nation was now ready to possess the land that God had made a covenant with Abraham, Isaac, and Jacob to give them the Promised Land flowing with milk and honey. Moses and Aaron had proven to them that God had sent them to bring them out of Egypt and the children of Israel were ready to follow them.

God's plan, that he told Moses to tell the house of Jacob and the children of Israel; you have seen what I have done to the Egyptians, and how I bare you on eagle's wings, and brought you unto myself. Now therefore, if you would obey my voice indeed, and keep my covenant, then you shall be a peculiar treasure unto me above all people: for all the earth is mine: You shall be unto me a kingdom of priests, and a holy nation. And all the people answered together, and said, "All that the LORD has spoken we will do."

After only three days into the wilderness the children of Israel began to murmur for lack of water, then they found the water at Marah, but it was bitter. They murmured more at Moses and he cried to the LORD and he told him to throw a certain tree into the water and it turned into sweet water. There he made for them a statute and an ordinance, and there he proved them, and said, if they would diligently hearken unto his voice and will do that which is right in his sight, and will give an ear to his commandments, and keep all his statutes, he will put none of the diseases upon you that he brought upon the Egyptians: for I am the LORD that heals you. And they came to Elim, where there were twelve wells of water and seventy palm trees and they camped by the waters. Then they went on to Wilderness of Sin on the fifteenth day of the second month after departing from Egypt. The whole congregation of the children of Israel murmured against Moses and Aaron about not enough food and that he was trying to kill them all with hunger.

This would be the first test to see if they would trust in God and listen diligently to his words and do, that which is right; instead of thinking how great it was when they were with the Gentiles in bondage.

God told Moses that he will rain bread from heaven for you and the people will go out and gather a certain rate every day which is one omer (2.08 quart) for every man, according to the number of persons in their tent, that I may prove them, whether they will walk in my law, or no. And it shall come to pass, that on the sixth days they will prepare that which they bring in; and it will be twice as much as they gather daily. If they measured the omers there should be enough but none left over. Moses and Aaron said unto all of them, This evening you shall know that the LORD brought you out of the land of Egypt: and in the morning, then you shall see the glory of the LORD; For that he hears your murmurings against the LORD: and what are we, that you murmur against us? The LORD told Moses that at even you shall eat flesh, and in the morning you shall be filled with bread; and you will know that I am the LORD your God. They called the little round bread, Manna. In the evening the quails came up and covered the camp.

Still there were people out there looking for bread on the seventh day, the Sabbath and there was none. They were to have gotten double on the sixth day so they would have it for the seventh day. They were to gather only one omer per man per day, and if they left it to morning, it would either stink or have worms, unless if was in the sixth night. There were those who didn't listen to that ordinance either. The LORD said to Moses, how long do you refuse to keep my commandments and my laws? They would eat manna from then until they came to the borders of the land of Canaan, which turned out to be forty years.

The children of Israel began to murmur again about water when they reached Rephidim and the Lord told Moses to strike the rock with his rod and water came out of the rock. And it was so. Then they tempted the LORD by saying, is the Lord with us, or not?

They then had to fight the Amaleks, Joshua chose some men and as long as Moses held his rod up then Israel would prevail and when his arms would go down the Amaleks would prevail. So Aaron and Hur held up his hands and Israel weaken them. Lord told Moses to write it as a memorial in the book and read it to Joshua, that the LORD would have war with them generation after generation.

Moses' father in law came with his daughter, Zipporah and Moses' children to hear all that had happened in Egypt. Jethro saw how long the days were with Moses judging all the people from daylight to night. The numbers of people were growing all the time. Jethro said, that was not good. So Jethro, the priest of Median, took a burnt offering and sacrifices to God and Moses and Aaron and the elders of Israel ate bread before God. Jethro said, I will give you counsel and told Moses to take the Chiefs of the already divided twelve tribes of Israel, and have them appoint heads over their people, captains over thousands, captains over hundreds, captains over fifty, captains over ten and officers among the tribes. They will judge all causes between their brethren and bring the hard causes to Moses. They will judge righteously and not respect persons. Jethro told them not to fear any mans face, for the judgment is God's. Each Chief of their tribe would choose their captains according to the number of men in the armies. He then said to Moses, and you shall teach them ordinances and laws, and shall show them the way they must walk, and the work they must do. Moreover you shall provide out of all the people able men, such as fear God, men of truth, hating covetousness; and place such over them as captains.

It was three months from when the children of Israel had come out of Egypt and they were in the desert of Sinai. Moses went up unto God, and the LORD called unto him out of the mountain, saying, Thus shall you say to the house of Jacob, and tell the children of Israel; you have seen what I did to the Egyptians, and how I bare you on eagles wings, and brought you unto myself. Now therefore, if you obey my voice indeed, and keep my covenant, then you shall be a peculiar treasure unto me above all people: for all the earth is mine: And you will be unto me a kingdom of priests, and a holy nation. These are the words, which you shall speak unto the children of Israel. Moses came and called the elders of the people and laid before their faces all the words that the LORD commanded him. And all the people answered together and said, All that the LORD has spoken we will do. And Moses returned the words of the people unto the LORD.

Moses had the elders to stay at the foot of the mount and wait for them to return. Moses and Joshua went up to the cloud that covered the mount; then God called Moses up into the mount and went into the cloud. He was there for six days and on the seventh day he called Moses out of the midst of the cloud for it was a day of rest. The children of Israel washed their clothes and were sanctified before God by the third day. The people could see the sight of glory on the top of the mount; it was like a devouring fire in their eyes. God spoke to them from the mount and the mount shook and the smoke was as from a furnace. God spoke all the Ten Commandments, the statutes and the judgments and they heard the thundering, and lightning, and the mountain smoking: and when they saw it, they removed themselves and stood far off. The people said to Moses, you speak to us, and we will hear: but let not God speak with us, lest we die. Moses said unto the people, fear not: for God has come to prove you, and that his fear may be before your face, that you sin not. Has The Lord talked to any that lived, other than us? The Lord then spoke all the judgments so they could judge the people with God's judgments. He also gave them the directions for the feast days and even clothes that the priests would wear and also the pattern for the tabernacle. Then he told Moses to take an offering from the people of the things needed for the tabernacle. Moses told the people that this is what the Lord commanded, saying take ye from among you an offering unto the Lord: whosoever is of a willing heart, let him bring it, an offering of the Lord; gold, and silver, and brass, and blue, and purple, and scarlet, and fine linen, and goats' hair, and rams' skins dyed red and badgers' skins, and shittim wood, and oil for the light, and spices for anointing oil, and for the breastplate. And every wise-hearted among you shall come, and make all that the Lord has commanded. And the people brought much more than enough for the service of the work.

And Moses did look upon all the work, and behold they had done it as the Lord had commanded, and Moses blessed them. And the Lord spoke to Moses and said on the first day of the first month shall you set up the tabernacle of the tent of the congregation. And thus Moses did all according to all that the Lord commanded him. And so it came to passing the first month in the second year, on the first day of the month that the tabernacle was reared up and brought the arc of the testimony into the tabernacle and set up the veil. So Moses finished the work. Then a cloud covered the tent of the congregation, and the glory of the LORD filled the tabernacle. Moses was not able to go into the tabernacle because the glory of the Lord filled the tabernacle. And when the cloud was taken up from over the tabernacle, the children of Israel went onward in all their journeys. But if the cloud were not taken up, then they journeyed not until it was taken up. For the cloud of the LORD was upon the tabernacle by day, and fire was on it at night, in the sight of all the house of Israel, throughout all their journeys. The LORD taught Moses all about the sacrifices necessary for the forgiveness of sins and it was taught to the children of Israel.

All the laws and judgments were written in the book of the covenant and ready; for the people had agreed to do all that the LORD set forth for them. Moses went up to the mount to get the covenant tables that God had prepared for putting into the ark. Moses was into the mount for forty days and forty nights.

The LORD said to Moses, "Go, get down there; for your people which you brought out of Egypt, have corrupted themselves: they have turned aside quickly out of the way which I commanded them: they have made them a molten calf, and have worshipped it, and have sacrificed thereunto, and said "These be the gods, O Israel, which have brought you out of Egypt". The LORD said, "I have seen these people and behold it is stiffnecked people: Now therefore leave me alone, that my wrath may wax hot against them, and I will consume them."

Moses besought The LORD his God, and said, "why? They are your people that you brought out of Egypt with great power and with a mighty hand? Wherefore shall the Egyptians speak and say, for mischief did he bring them out, to slay them in the mountains, and consume them from the face of the earth? Turn from thy fierce wrath, and repent of this evil against your people". *"Remember Abraham, Isaac, and Israel, thy servants, to whom thou swore by thine own self, and said unto them I will multiply you seed as the stars of heaven, and all this land that I have spoken of will I give unto your seed, they shall inherit it for ever."*

The LORD repented of the evil that he thought to do unto his people.

Moses went down from the mount and saw the calf and threw the tables onto the ground and they broke. He took the calf and broke it and burned it into powder and threw it upon the water and made the children of Israel drink of it. When he saw that they were naked he asked, who is on the LORD's side? All the sons of Levi gathered themselves unto him. And he said, thus said the LORD God of Israel, Put every man his sword by his side and go in and out of the gate to gate through out the camp, slay every man his brother, and every man his companion and every man his neighbor. And the children of Levi did according to the word of Moses: and there fell of the people that day about three thousand men.

Moses returned to the LORD and said, this people have sinned a great sin, and have made them gods of gold. Moses asked God to blot his name out of his book and forgive them their sin. He offered himself for their forgiveness.

The Lord answered, whoever has sinned against me will I blot out of my book. Therefore now go, lead the people unto the place of which I have spoken unto you: behold mine Angel shall go before you, nevertheless in the day when I visit I will visit their sin upon them. The LORD said I will send an angel before you and I will drive out Canaanite, the Amorite, and the Hittite, and the Perizzite, the Hivite, and the Jebusite: unto the land flowing with milk and honey: for I will not go up in the midst of thee; for though art a stiffneck people: lest I consume you on the way. When the people heard they mourned.

Moses prayed you have said, I know you by name, and I have found grace in thy sight. Now, therefore I pray thee, if I have found grace in your sight, show me thy way, that I may know you, that I might find grace in your sight: and consider that this nation is your people.

And the LORD *said*, "My presence shall go with you, and I will give you rest". And *Moses* said; if your presence goes not with me, carry us not up hence. For wherein shall it be known here that I and thy people have found grace in thy sight? Is it not that you go with us? So shall we be separated, I and thy people, from all the people that are upon the face of the earth.

And the *Lord* said unto Moses, I will do this thing also that thou has spoken: for thou has found grace in my sight, and I know you by name.

Moses said, I beseech thee, show me your glory.

The Lord said, I will make all my goodness pass before you. And the Lord passed by before him and I will proclaim the name of the Lord before you; and will be gracious to whom I will be gracious, and will show mercy on whom I will show mercy. You cannot see my face: for there shall no man see me and live. I will put you in a cleft in the rock and you shall see only my back parts. The skin of Moses' face shone that the people were afraid of him and he had to put a veil over his face when he talked to them.

The Lord told him to hew thee two tables of stone like unto the first: and he will write upon these tables the words that were in the first tables, which you broke. Be ready in the morning, and come up in the morning unto mount Sinai, and present thyself there to me on the top of the mount. And no man shall come up with thee, neither let any man be seen throughout the entire mount; neither let any flocks or herds feed before that mount.

Moses took the tables and got up early and went to the Lord and he descended in a cloud and stood with him there, and proclaimed the name of the Lord. And the Lord passed by before him and proclaimed," The Lord, the Lord God, merciful and gracious, longsuffering, and abundant in goodness and truth, keeping mercy for thousands, forgiving iniquity and transgression and sin, and that will by no means clear the guilty; visiting the iniquity of the fathers upon the children unto the third and fourth generation".

And Moses hurried and bowed his head toward the earth, and worshipped. And he said, if now I have found grace in thy sight, O Lord, let my Lord, I pray thee, go among us; for it is a stiffnecked people; and pardon our iniquity and our sin, and take us for thine inheritance.

We can only imagine this relationship between God and Moses at this particular time in history. We know that he lived for forty years with Jethro, a priest of Midian. How convenient for a man who was brought up as an Egyptian and knows the language; then runs away only to come to live in Median with a Godly Priest. And also to be taught many things about his Hebrew heritage and the language from, his brother, Aaron, so that he could eventually be used by God to go and bring the Hebrew people out of Egypt. And Moses he was eighty years old when he went to talk to Pharaoh and his brother; Aaron was eighty-three years old.

God's love for Moses brought him to make another covenant with the children of Israel. He told him that they should worship no other god: for the LORD, whose name is Jealous, is a jealous God.

PART TWO

GOD PREPARING FOR THE
HOLY ONE

CHAPTER 7

THE FOUNDATIONS
OF GOD

GOD'S EARTH AND HEAVENS FOUNDATION

And, Thou, Lord, in the beginning hast laid the foundation of the earth; and the heavens are the works of thine hands. Of old thou has laid the foundation of the earth: and the heavens are the work of thy hands. His foundation is in the holy mountains.

Great is the LORD, and greatly to be praised in the city of our God, in the mountain of his holiness. Thus said God the LORD, "he that created the heavens, and stretched them out; he that spread forth the earth, and that which comes out of it; he that give breath unto the people upon it, and spirit to them that walk therein." Mine hand also hath laid the foundation of the earth, and my right hand hath spanned the heavens: when I call unto them, they stand up together.

Then shall the King say unto them on his right hand, Come, you blessed of my Father, inherit the kingdom prepared for you from the foundation of the world.

SOLOMON'S TEMPLE FOUNDATION

Thou know how that King David my father could not build an house unto the name of the LORD his God for the wars which were about him on every side, until the LORD put them under the soles of his feet. But now the LORD my God hath given me rest on every side, so that there is neither adversary nor evil. And, behold, I purpose to build an house unto the Name of the LORD my God, as the LORD spoke unto King David my father, saying, Thy son, whom I will set upon thy throne in thy room, he shall build an house unto my Name.

And he appointed, according to the order of David his father, the courses of the priests to their service, and the Levites to their charges, to praise and minister before the priests, as the duty of every day required: the porters also by their courses at every gate: for so had David the man of God commanded. And they departed not from the commandment of the king unto the priests and Levites concerning any matter, or concerning the treasures. And King Solomon commanded, and they brought great stones, costly stones, and hewed stones, to *lay the foundation of the house.*

Now all the work of Solomon was prepared for unto the day of the *foundation of the house of the* LORD, and until it was finished. So the house of the LORD was perfected.

In the fourth year was the foundation of the house of the LORD laid, in the month Zif:

Then Solomon began to build the house of the LORD at Jerusalem in mount Moriah, where the LORD appeared unto David his father, in the place that David had prepared in the threshing floor of Ornan the Jebusite.

And it came to pass in the four hundred and eightieth year after the children of Israel were come out of the land of Egypt, in the fourth year of Solomon's reign over Israel, in the month Zif, which is the second month, that he began to build the house of the LORD. And in the eleventh year, in the month Bul, which is the eighth month, was the house finished throughout all the parts thereof, and according to all the fashion of it. So was he seven years in building it. And the word of the LORD came to Solomon, saying, "Concerning this house which thou art in building, if thou wilt walk in my statutes, and execute my judgments, and keep all my commandments to walk in them; then will I perform my word with thee, which I spoke unto David thy father: And I will dwell among the children of Israel, and will not forsake my people Israel. So Solomon built the house, and finished it.(about 960 BC) It was totally destroyed by Babylon in about 586 BC

ZERUBBABEL'S TEMPLE FOUNDATION

Thy throne, O God, is forever and ever: the sceptre of thy kingdom is a right *sceptre* (staff).

Now the sons of Reuben the firstborn of Israel, (for he was the firstborn; but, forasmuch as he defiled his father's bed, his birthright was given unto the sons of Joseph the son of Israel: and the *genealogy is not to be reckoned after the birthright*. For *Judah* prevailed above his brethren, and of him came the chief ruler; but the birthright was Joseph's.

The *sceptre* shall not depart from Judah, nor a lawgiver from between his feet, until Shiloh come; and unto him shall the gathering of the people be. But unto the Son he said, Thy throne, O God, is forever and ever: a *sceptre* of righteousness is the *sceptre* of thy kingdom.

And Judah saw there a daughter of a certain Canaanite, whose name was Shuah; and he took her, as wife and went in unto her. Time passes and Judah took a wife for Er his firstborn, her name was Tamar. But Er, was wicked in the sight of the LORD; and the LORD slew him. And Judah said unto Onan, his second son, "Go in unto thy brother's wife, and marry her, and raise up seed to thy brother". And the thing, which he did, displeased the LORD: wherefore he slew him also.

Judah had then lost his Canaanite wife and the two sons that had married Tamar, so he sent her home till his last son was old enough to marry.

He did not intend to do so. Tamar wanted a son for to take care of and care for her in her old age and God wanted a son for the lineage of His Son. And it was told Tamar, saying, "Behold thy father in law going up to Timnath to shear his sheep," And she put her widow's garments off from her, and covered her with a vail, and wrapped herself, and sat in an open place, which is by the way to Timnath; for she saw that Shelah was grown, and she was not given unto him to wife. When Judah saw her, he thought her to be a harlot; because she had covered her face. And he turned unto her by the way, and said, go to, I pray thee, let me come in unto thee; (for he knew not that she was his daughter in law.) And she said, "What will thou give me, that thou may come in unto me? And he said, "I will send thee a kid from the flock". And she said, "Will thou give me *a pledge*, till thou send it"? And he said, "What pledge shall I give thee"? And *she said, "Thy signet (ring), and thy bracelets, and thy staff that is in your hand". And he gave it her, and came in unto her, and she conceived by him.* And Judah sent the kid by the hand of his friend the Adullamite, to receive his pledge from the woman's hand: but he found her not. Then he asked the men of that place, saying, "Where is the harlot, that was openly by the way side"? And they said, "There was no harlot in this place".

And he returned to Judah, and said, I cannot find her; and also the men of the place said, that there was no harlot in this place.

And Judah said, Let her take it to her, *lest we be shamed*: behold, I sent this kid, and thou hast not found her.

And it came to pass about three months after, that it was told Judah, saying, " Tamar thy daughter in law hath played the harlot; and also, behold, she is with child by whoredom." And Judah said, "Bring her forth, and let her be burnt." When she was brought forth, she sent to her father in law, saying, "By the man, whose these are, am I with child: and she said, Discern, I pray thee, whose are these, *the signet,* and *bracelets,* and *staff (sceptre)*".

And Judah acknowledged them, and said, "She hath been more righteous than I; because that I gave her not to Shelah my son." And he knew her again no more. Tamar gave Judah twins and both are listed in the genealogy of Jesus.

The sceptre shall not depart from Judah, nor a lawgiver from between his feet, until Shiloh come; and unto him shall the gathering of the people be.

That which is written of Cyrus: "He is my shepherd, and shall perform all my pleasure: even saying to Jerusalem, Thou shall be built; and to the temple, thy foundation shall be laid" Thus said the Lord to his anointed, to Cyrus, whose right hand I have holden. For Jacob my servant's sake, and Israel mine elect, I have even called thee by thy name: I have surnamed thee, though thou hast not known me. I am the LORD, and there is none else, there is no God beside me: I girded thee, though thou hast not known me: That they may know from the rising of the sun, and from the west, that there is none beside me. I am the LORD, and there is none else.

Therefore thus said the Lord GOD, Behold, I lay in Zion for a *foundation a stone,* a *tried stone, a* precious corner stone, *a sure foundation*: he that believes shall not make haste. *Judgment* also will I lay to the *line,* and righteousness to the plummet: and the hail shall sweep away the refuge of lies, and the waters shall overflow the hiding place.

In the first year of Cyrus the king the same Cyrus the king made a decree concerning the house of God at Jerusalem, Let the house be built, the place where they offered sacrifices, and let the *foundations thereof be strongly laid;* the height thereof threescore cubits, and the breadth thereof threescore cubits; And the *vessels also of gold and silver of the house of God,* which Nebuchadnezzar took out of the temple that was in Jerusalem, and brought them into the temple of Babylon, those did *Cyrus the king* take out of the temple of Babylon, and they were delivered unto one, whose name was *Sheshbazzar*, whom *he* had made *governor*. Even those did Cyrus king of Persia bring forth by the hand of Mithredath the treasurer, and numbered them unto *Sheshbazzar, the prince of Judah*. (Persian for Zerubbabel) All the vessels of gold and of silver were five thousand and four hundred. All these did Sheshbazzar bring up with them of the captivity that were brought up from Babylon unto Jerusalem. And while the builders laid the *foundation of the temple of the* LORD, they set the priests in their apparel with trumpets, and the Levites the sons of Asaph with cymbals, to praise the LORD, after the ordinance of David king of Israel. And they sang together by course in praising and giving thanks unto the LORD; because he is good, for his mercy endures forever toward Israel. Then came the same *Sheshbazzar, and laid the foundation of the house of God*, which is in Jerusalem: and since that time even until now hath it been in building, and yet it is not finished.

But all the people shouted with a great shout, when they praised the LORD, because the *foundation of the house of the* LORD *was laid*. But many of the priests and Levites and chief of the fathers, who were ancient men, that had seen the first house, when the foundation of this house was laid before their eyes, wept with a loud voice; and many shouted aloud for joy:

In the second year of Darius the king, in the sixth month, in the first day of the month, came the word of the LORD by Haggai the prophet unto *Zerubbabel* the son of Shealtiel, *governor of Judah*, and to *Joshua the son of Josedech, the high priest*, saying, "Thus speaks the LORD of hosts, saying, this people say, the time are not come, the time that the LORD's house should be built.

In the seventh month, in the one and twentieth day of the month, came the *word of the* LORD by the prophet Haggai, saying, Speak now to Zerubbabel the son of Shealtiel, governor of Judah, and to Joshua the son of Josedech, the high priest, and to the residue of the people, saying, "Who is left among you that saw this house in her first glory"? And how do you see it now? Is it not in your eyes in comparison of it as nothing? *Yet now be strong, O Zerubbabel, said the* LORD; and be strong, O Joshua, son of Josedech, the high priest; and be strong, all you people of the land, said the LORD, and work: for I am with you, said the LORD of hosts.

Thus said the LORD of hosts; "Let your hands be strong, you that hear in these days these words by the mouth of the prophets, which were in *the day that the foundation of the house of the* LORD *of hosts was laid,* that the *temple might be built.* Now therefore thus saith the LORD of hosts; consider your ways. Because of mine house that is waste, and you run every man unto his own house. Go up to the mountain, and bring wood, and build the house; and I will take pleasure in it, and I will be glorified, saith the LORD. Then *Zerubbabel* the son of Shealtiel, and *Joshua* the son of Josedech, the high priest, with all the remnant of the people, obeyed the voice of the LORD their God, and the words of Haggai the prophet, as the LORD their God had sent him, and the people did fear before the LORD. Then spoke Haggai the LORD's messenger in the LORD's *message unto the people, saying, I am with you, saith the* LORD. *And the* LORD *stirred up the spirit of Zerubbabel the son of Shealtiel, governor of Judah, and the spirit of Joshua the son of Josedech, the high priest, and the spirit of all the remnant of the people; and they came and did work in the house of the* LORD *of hosts, their God,* Consider now *from this day and upward,* from the four and twentieth day of the ninth month, even from the day that the *foundation of the* LORD's *temple* was laid, consider it.

In that day, said the LORD of hosts, "I will take thee, O Zerubbabel, my servant, the son of Shealtiel, said the LORD, and will make thee as a *signet*: for I have chosen thee, said the Lord *of hosts*. Speak to Zerubbabel, governor of Judah, saying, *"I will shake the heavens and the earth. And I will overthrow the throne of kingdoms, and I will destroy the strength of the kingdoms of the heathen; and I will overthrow the chariots, and those that ride in them; and the horses and their riders shall come down, every one by the sword of his brother.".* This is the *word of the* Lord *unto Zerubbabel,* saying, *"*Not by might, nor by power, but by my spirit, said the Lord of hosts. Who art thou, O great mountain? Before Zerubbabel thou shall become a plain: and he shall bring forth the headstone thereof with shoutings, crying, Grace, grace unto it. Moreover the word of the Lord came unto me, saying, *the hands of Zerubbabel have laid the foundation of this house; his hands shall also finish it; and thou shall know that the* Lord *of hosts hath sent me unto you.* For who hath despised the day of small things? "For they shall rejoice, and *shall see the plummet in the hand of Zerubbabel with those seven; they are the eyes of the* Lord, *which run to and fro through the whole earth.* And the elders of the Jews builded, and they prospered through the prophesying of Haggai the prophet and Zechariah the son of Iddo. And they builded, and finished it, according to the commandment of the God of Israel, and according to the commandment of Cyrus, and Darius, and Artaxerxes king of Persia. And this house was finished on the third day of the month Adar, which was in the sixth year of the reign of Darius the king in 516B.C.

(Heb 1:8 But unto the Son he says, "Thy throne, O God, is for ever and ever: a sceptre of righteousness is the sceptre of thy kingdom." This highly holy building of the foundation of the second temple became the same foundation that the Messiah would walk on so many years later. Zerubbabel was the Governor and Prince of Judah who laid the foundation, built the temple and was chosen as a signet to bring the Messiah into the midst of his people. King Jehoiachin was the last king of Judah. There would be no more kings of Judah in the line of David until Lord Jesus Christ comes as the King of kings and Lord of lords.

The temple had deteriorated over the approximate 496 years and was rebuilt; and made ready on the same foundation built by Zerubbabel; by Herod the Great in 20 Bc.

After the resurrection of Christ, they would have to wait for God's right time for the mystery of the foundation of Jesus Christ and how he can build a living temple by the gospel of God given to the Apostle Paul by resurrected Son of God.

Paul Builds on Gods Foundation:

For man can lay no other foundation than that which is laid, which is Jesus Christ.

But you are a chosen generation, a royal priesthood, an holy nation, a peculiar people; that you should show forth the praises of him who has called you out of darkness into his marvelous light:

Which in time past were not a people, but are now the people of God: which had not obtained mercy, but now have obtained mercy.

As the whirlwind passes, so is the wicked no more: but the *righteous is an everlasting foundation.*

Now therefore you are no more strangers and foreigners, but fellow citizens with the saints, and of the household of God; And are built upon the foundation of the apostles and prophets, Jesus Christ himself being the chief corner stone; In whom all the building fitly framed together grows unto an holy temple in the Lord: In whom you also are built together for an habitation of God through the Spirit. Paul spoke to the Gentiles and said,

"For this cause I Paul, the prisoner of Jesus Christ for you Gentiles, if you have heard of the dispensation of the grace of God which is given me to you-ward: How that by revelation he made known unto me the mystery, which in other ages was not made known unto the sons of men, as the Spirit now revealed it unto his holy apostles and prophets; That the Gentiles should be fellow heirs, and of the same body, and partakers of his promise in Christ by the gospel: whereof I was made a minister, according to the *gift of the grace of God* given unto me by the effectual working of his power. Unto me, who am less than the least of all saints, is this grace given, that I should preach among the Gentiles the unsearchable riches of Christ; And to make all men see what is the fellowship of the *mystery*, which from the beginning of the world hath been *hid in God, who created all things by Jesus Christ.*

God's plan has always been the remission of sin and all men would see the fellowship of the mystery through the foundation of Jesus Christ. These are Paul's teachings:

For we are laborers together with God: you are God's husbandry, you are God's building.

According to the grace of God, which is given unto me, as a wise *master builder, I have laid* the *foundation*, and another builds thereon. But let every man take heed how he builds there upon. For other *foundation* can no man lay than that is laid, *which is Jesus Christ.*

Now if any man builds upon this foundation gold, silver, precious stones, wood, hay, and stubble. Every man's work shall be made manifest: for the day shall declare it, because it shall be revealed by fire; and the fire shall try every man's work of what sort it is. If any man's work *abides* which he hath built thereupon, he shall receive a reward. If any man's work shall be *burned,* he shall suffer loss: *but* he himself shall be *saved;* yet so as by fire.

Know you not that you are the temple of God, and that the Spirit of God dwells in you?

If any man defile the temple of God, him shall God destroy; for the temple of God is holy, which temple you are.

And you are Christ's; and Christ is God's.

PARABLE EXAMPLES:

Whosoever comes to me, and hears my sayings, and does them, I will show you to whom he is like: He is like a man which built an house, and dug deep, and laid the *foundation on a rock*: and when the flood arose, the stream beat vehemently upon that house, and could not shake it: for it was founded upon a rock.

But he that hears, and does not, is like a man that *without a foundation*, built a house upon the earth; against which the stream did beat vehemently, and immediately it fell; and the ruin of that house was great.

For which of you, intending to build a tower, sits not down first, and counts the cost, whether he has sufficient to finish it?

Lest haply, after he hath laid the foundation, and is not able to finish it, all that behold it begin to mock him, Saying, This man began to build, and was not able to finish.

PAUL'S DOCTRINE:

God that made the world and all things therein, seeing that he is Lord of heaven and earth, dwells not in temples made with hands; And hath made of one blood all nations of men for to dwell on all the face of the earth, and hath determined the times before appointed, and the bounds of their habitation; That they should seek the Lord, if haply they might feel after him, and find him, though he be not far from every one of us: For in him we live, and move, and have our being; as certain also of your own poets have said, For we are also his offspring. Forasmuch then as we are the offspring of God, we ought not to think that the Godhead is like unto gold, or silver, or stone, graven by art and man's device.

And the times of this ignorance God winked at; but *now commanded* all men every where to repent: Because he hath *appointed a day*, in the which he will *judge the world in righteousness* by that man whom he hath ordained; whereof he hath given assurance unto all men, in that he had *raised him from the dead.*

Saul had been told at the second encounter with Jesus, "But rise, and stand upon thy feet: for I have appeared unto thee for this purpose, to make thee a minister and a witness both of these things which thou hast seen, and of those things in the which I will appear unto thee; Delivering thee from the people, and from the Gentiles, unto whom now I send thee, To open their eyes, and to turn them from darkness to light, and from the power of Satan unto God, that they may receive forgiveness of sins, and inheritance among them which are sanctified by faith that is in me.

But showed first unto them of Damascus, this was the beginning of a new man called Paul the Apostle; then at Jerusalem, and throughout all the coasts of Judea, and then to the Gentiles, that they should repent and turn to God, and do works meet for repentance. For these causes the *Jews* caught him in the temple, and went about *to kill me*. Having therefore obtained help of God, I continue unto this day, witnessing both to small and great, saying none other things than those, which the prophets and Moses did say, should come: That Christ should suffer, and that he should be the first that should rise from the dead, and should show light unto the people, and to the Gentiles.

For none of us lives to himself, and no man dies to himself. For whether we live, we live unto the Lord; and whether we die, we die unto the Lord: whether we live therefore, or die, we are the Lord's.

For to this end Christ both died, and rose, and revived, that he might be Lord both of the dead and living. For we are his workmanship, created in Christ Jesus unto good works, which God hath before ordained that we should walk in them.

Wherefore remember, that you being in time past Gentiles in the flesh, who are called Uncircumcision by that which is called the Circumcision in the flesh made by hands;

That at that time you were without Christ, being aliens from the commonwealth of Israel, and strangers from the covenants of promise, having no hope, and without God in the world:

But now in *Christ Jesus*, you who were sometimes far off are made nigh by the blood of Christ.

For he is our peace, who hath made both one, and hath broken down the middle wall of partition between us and God; having abolished in his flesh the enmity, even the law of commandments contained in ordinances; for to make *in himself* of twain one new man, so making peace;

And that he might reconcile both *unto God in one body by the cross*, having slain the enmity thereby: And came and preached peace to you which were afar off, and to them that were nigh.

For through him we both have access by one Spirit unto the Father.

Now therefore you are no more strangers and foreigners, but fellow citizens with the saints, and of the household of God; and are built upon the foundation of Jesus Christ. In whom all the building fitly framed together grows unto a holy temple in the Lord: In whom you also are built together for an habitation of God through the Spirit.

NEW JERUSALEM FOUNDATIONS:

And I *John* saw the holy city, New Jerusalem, coming down from God out of heaven, prepared as a bride adorned for her husband.

And the wall of the city had *twelve foundations*, and in them the names of the twelve apostles of the Lamb. And the *foundations* of the wall of the city were garnished with all manner of precious stones. *The first foundation* was jasper; the *second*, sapphire; the *third*, a chalcedony; the *fourth*, an emerald; The *fifth*, sardonyx; the *sixth*, sardius; the *seventh*, chrysolite; the *eighth*, beryl; the *ninth*, a topaz; the *tenth*, a chrysoprasus; the *eleventh*, a jacinth; the *twelfth*, an amethyst.

And I saw *no temple* therein: *for the Lord God Almighty and the Lamb are the temple of it.*

And the Spirit and the bride say, Come. And let him that hears say, Come. And let him that is athirst come. And whosoever will, let him take the water of life freely. For I testify unto every man that hears the words of the prophecy of this book, If any man shall add unto these things, God shall add unto him the plagues that are written in this book: And if any man shall take away from the words of the book of this prophecy, God shall take away his part out of the book of life, and out of the holy city, and from the things which are written in this book.

He, who testifies these things, says, "Surely I come quickly." Amen.

Even so, come, Lord Jesus. The grace of our Lord Jesus Christ be with you all. Amen.

CHAPTER 8

WOMEN AND WIDOWS OF GOD

Honor all men. Love the brotherhood. Fear God. Honor the king.

For you were as sheep going astray; but are now returned unto the Shepherd and Bishop of your souls.

Likewise, you wives, be in subjection to your own husbands; that, if any not obey the word, they may also without the word be won by the conversation of the wives; while they behold your chaste conversation coupled with fear. For after this manner in the old time the holy women also, who trusted in God, adorned themselves, being in subjection unto their own husbands.

Anna, wife of Heli:

Anna, who was born in about 57 Bc, married Heli, a Levite in about 42BC. They named their daughter who was born in about 41BC, Mary, knowing that they were the last in the line for the virgin to bring in the Holy One of Israel. They believed that this was she; but it was not in God's timing. (*This would be too early for the Messiah because the temple would not begin to be rebuilt upon the same Zerubbabel's foundation, until 20BC by Herod the Great.*) Mary, at the time of her betrothal, had not been prepared by an angel; so did not have a virgin birth. She married Cleophas her betrothed and conceived a daughter, Salome. God has always made a way upfront and it passes down through the generations so we may think that we missed their plan A. I believe that this one gave God pleasure, being they did not give up and waited for another child. (To have so many "Mary's " during his Son's earthly ministry and secret ways to find out which one would be his beautiful Plan B. But as Ishmael had been taken care of by God, so it was with Anna's first daughter, Mary, wife of Cleopus (Alpheus). She was given two daughters and five sons. Of her sons, four became Apostles of Jesus; they were Mathew, James, Jude, and Simon. The fifth son, Joses (Barnabus) was a disciple of Jesus and Paul the Apostle. The first daughter of Mary, wife of Cleophas, was Salome who married Zebedee and birthed two sons, John and James, who also became Apostles of Jesus. The Mary, wife of Cleophas, decided to name her second daughter, Mary *I think we can see why* but she was betrothed and married to Simon Peter, another man who became an Apostle of Jesus and they had a son Marcus who was a disciple of both Jesus and Paul.

After a long time, around forty years after their first daughter, in God's timing, Heli and Anna had a second daughter and called her Mary and this time the angel appeared to her and said that she was the virgin that God had chosen and in God's timing to bring into the world, the Messiah.

Both women, Anna and Elisabeth were past the childbirth age and they brought into the world the Holy One and the last Great Prophet.

How could this have come about? We tend to forget that our GOD is an awesome GOD and all things are possible with our God. We are in this fallen world and we are subject to physical death; and most of us before even one century. God had been following His own Plan of Redemption for many, many centuries. We should understand why God said," *My thoughts are not your thoughts, neither are your ways my ways. For the heavens are higher than the earth, so are my ways higher than your ways, and my thoughts than your thoughts."* (*Isaiah 55:9*) God was and is and forever will be. How could even the most wise man on earth compare himself to the Almighty GOD? Never happen! We need to humble ourselves before God and He will give you priceless wisdom and love, which brings true humility and a life of abundance.

Many have just ignored *John 19:25 "Now stood by the cross of Jesus his mother, and his mother's sister, Mary the wife of Cleophas and Mary Magdalene."*

Others have not recognized this scripture so they said "Jesus' mother married Cleophas after Joseph died". If that were so, being that Joseph was last spoken of when Jesus was twelve years old and his mother was alone when he began his ministry at thirty years of age. That still doesn't answer *John 19:25* if it had been her sister who married Cleophas and we would have to wonder why Jesus would have to give his mother to John and move her into his house if she already had a husband.

Others have yet decided to give the Virgin Mary many children after Jesus; it would have had to be multiple births for all the sons of Mary to have been of age to minister to the children of Israel. John the Baptist was also thirty years old when he began his ministry. The Jewish law states they would have to be thirty years or older and Jesus and John the Baptist were thirty when they began their ministries. Jesus was the minister of the Jews and had to obey the Law.

All of the Apostles would have to have been thirty years old or older for Jesus to send them out to minister on their own as he did or the Sanhedrin would have had reason to stop Him for breaking the Law.

Many have also been unable to figure *Luke 7: 12-15* because of ignoring *John 19:25*. Why did Jesus just out of the way and go to Nain to rise up a dead only son of a widow? It is well known in their culture that widows with no sons were left to have very difficult lives.

The LORD also showed us with Naomi and Ruth when he had compassion on both of these widows, when they trusted God. It was the knowing of Jesus that his mother would also be a widow without a son in a very short time that led him to Nain.

(*1 Kings 17:9-24*) God has shown through Elijah when God sent him to the city of Zarephath to a starving widow and her son. She believed and obeyed the word of the LORD and she gave their last meal to Elijah and the LORD provided her enough to sustain the three of them until the famine was over.

And it came to pass after these things, that the son of the woman, the mistress of the house, fell sick; and his sickness was so sore, that there was no breath left in him. And she said unto Elijah, "What have I to do with thee, O thou man of God?" art thou come unto me to call my sin to remembrance, and to slay my son? And he said unto her, "Give me thy son." And he took him out of her bosom, and carried him up into a loft, where he abode, and laid him upon his own bed.

And he cried unto the LORD, and said, "O LORD my God, hast thou also brought evil upon the widow with whom I sojourn, by slaying her son?" And he stretched himself upon the child three times, and cried unto the LORD, and said, "O LORD my God, I pray thee, let this child's soul come into him again." And the LORD heard the voice of Elijah; and the soul of the child came into him again, and he revived. And Elijah took the child, and brought him down out of the chamber into the house, and delivered him unto his mother: and Elijah said, "See, thy son lives."

And the woman said to Elijah, "Now by this I know that thou art a man of God, and that the word of the LORD in thy mouth is truth."

This is another one of the many questions in the sorting of the Who's who.

Why did Jesus give his mother to John the son of Zebedee as his mother? He was there comforting his mother at the cross.

And also because John son of Zebedee was the Apostle that Jesus loved, and he was in the bloodline of Heli through Salome, daughter of Mary, the wife of Cleophas. God chose him because he was not finished with him and He seemed to have a heart for the youngest.

All through the scriptures God has had a heart for women who trust in Him. He created them with strength and courage as we saw in Sarah, who gave birth at ninety but also a humbleness that gave her a respect for the anointing of God. Hagar who was sent away with her son into the wilderness listened to the LORD and was shown the way to their destiny.

The LORD told Rebeckah who had twin boys, that the older would serve the younger. She had the courage and strength to deceive her husband so what God said would come true knowing she would never see Jacob the son she loved ever again while she lived. Leah, whose father deceived Jacob into a marriage to Leah instead of Rachel whom he loved and thought he had married. Leah felt that her husband did not love her. He loved Rachel so God gave Leah children because she was not loved. Finally Rachel had Joseph and then died in Benjamin's birth. Through all the hardships of Jacob's women, all four of them had managed to come together as a family and give him the twelve princes of Israel.

Another woman of the most fortitude was able to perceive the anointing upon Elisha as he walked through Shunem. The Shunammite woman stepped forward as he was passing through Shunem and the great woman constrained him to come and have bread with her. There was a spiritual bond between Elisha and the Shunammite, and so it was, that as often that he came he turned in to eat bread. She said to her husband, I perceive that this is a holy man of God, which passes by us continually. Let us make a little chamber, I pray thee, on the wall; and let us set for him there a bed, and a table, and a stool, and a candlestick: and it shall be, when he comes to us, that he will turn in there. It came a day and he came there and turned into the chamber and lay there. He told his servant to call her and say you have cared well for us. "What is to be done for you? Would you be spoken for to the King or captain of the host?" She answered, I dwell among mine own people. The servant said, "she has no child and her husband is old." Elisha said to her, "this season, according to the time of life, you shall embrace a son." She said, "Nay, my lord, thou man of God, do not lie to thy handmaid." And the woman did conceive and bare a son at the season that Elisa had said to her. When the child was grown, he went out with his dad to the reaper one day and then told his dad that his head hurt. He told one of the young men to carry him to his mother. *He sat on her lap till noon and died.* She went up and laid him on the bed of the man of God and closed the door. She called her husband and said, "send me, I pray thee, and one of the young men and one of the donkeys that I may run to the man of God, and come again." Her husband said, "It is not the new moon or the Sabbath." She said, "*It shall be well.*" She told her servant drive and slack not unless I tell you. She went and came unto the man of God at Mt. Carmel. When the man of God saw her at a distance, he told his servant, behold yonder is that Shunammite. Run now I pray thee and *ask her if all is well with her, her husband and the child.* She answered, "*It is well*". And when she came to the man of God to the hill, she caught him at his feet and the servant was going to push her away. But the man of God said "Let her alone for *her soul is vexed within her and the* LORD *has hid it from me, and has not told me*". He then told the servant to take his staff and lay it on the child's face. The mother of the child said, "*As the* LORD *lives, and as thy soul lives, I will not leave thee*". And he arose and followed her. The servant went ahead but laying the staff on the child's face did not awaken him. *Elisha* went into the house and *lay upon the child until his flesh was warm.* Then he went out and came back in the house and *walked to and fro*; he then *stretched himself upon him and he sneezed seven times, and opened his eyes.* He told his servant to call the Shunammite. When she came in he said" take up thy son". *She fell at his feet and bowed herself to the ground, took up her son and went out.*

There was a war over in Syria and Jerusalem so Elisha was gone for a while. When God told *Elisha* that there was going to be *seven years of famine in the land,* he went and *told the Shunammite* saying "arise you and your household and *sojourn in the land of the Philistines for the seven years." The woman did what the man of God said.*

It came to pass, after the seven years she returned out of the land of the Philistines and found that people had taken her house and land: and *she went forth to cry to the king for her house and for her land. At that same time the servant of Elisha was with the king telling him about what Elisha had done for the Shunammite and her son and the King asked if all these things were true?* He told the King, yes they are true and she came into the King and the servant said, this is the woman and this is her son that Elisha restored to life. So the King appointed unto her a certain officer saying *Restore all that was hers, and all the fruits of the field since the day she left the land, even until now.*

It is so like our God to ask what do we want and we say we don't need it, but down the road we just happen to need that very thing and he has it waiting for us. Elisha had asked her if he could speak to the King for her and she refused. Now when she needed him to speak for her, he had already taken care of it before she arrived. She also would not speak that her son was dead, which is a picture of the trust she had put in the man of God's teachings at time for bread and the honor she had for her husband. He did not question her, he just trusted her.

We serve an awesome God. Most women today would like to see their husbands so anointed that they can see God working in them. There is no greater love for a godly woman than to have a husband who loves her as Christ loves the church; which was so much that he gave his life for Church.

CHAPTER 9

JESUS THE CHRIST'S FAMILY GENEALOGY

The Messiah was to come from the line of David according to the scriptures. And this is the book of the genealogy that was planned by God in preparation for His Son. Jacob spoke over Judah: "*The sceptre shall not depart from Judah, nor a lawgiver from between his feet, until Shiloh come; and unto him shall the gathering of the people be.*" So all the Old Covenant scriptures of the Law of Moses and of the prophets and the Psalms were just a shadow that would be fulfilled when the Messiah came. But now hath he obtained a more excellent ministry, by how much also he is the mediator of a better covenant, which was established upon better promises. For if that first covenant had been faultless, then should no place have been sought for the second. For finding fault with them, he said, Behold, the day's come, said the Lord, when I will make a new covenant with the house of Israel and with the house of Judah. For if that first covenant had been faultless, then there should be no reason to have been sought for the second covenant. Not according to the covenant that I made with their fathers in the day when I took them by the hand to lead them out of the land of Egypt; because they continued not in my covenant, and I regarded them not, said the Lord. And these are the days that

Israel had been waiting for, and that the Gentiles might glorify God for his mercy; as it is written, "For this cause I will confess to thee among the Gentiles and sing unto thy name. And again, Praise the Lord, all you Gentiles and praise him all nations." For God so loved the world that he gave the world his only begotten Son that WHOSOEVER believes in Him should not perish but have everlasting life. Now I Paul say that Jesus Christ was a minister of the circumcision for the truth of God, to confirm the promises made unto the fathers.

Heli (Eli in Hebrew) and Anna were Levites from the line of David and through *Zerubbabel*, which was his Hebrew name and who was the chosen one of God. He had two other names also, *Zorobabel* (Greek), *Sheshbazzar* (Persian) the prince of Judah; Many generations had passed from but they carried the signet for the man who would birth the woman who would give birth to the promised one. Now it was passed unto the last of the line, which were Heli and his wife Anna who were married in Gods good timing, which was about forty-two B.C. When they brought forth a daughter in about forty-one B.C., they believed that this would be the promised virgin and named her Mary. They watched her grow expectantly and taught her all about the Law of Moses. When she was of age, they betrothed her to Alphaeus (Cleophas or Cleopas) in about twenty-three B.C., a very godly man. They waited expectantly during the betrothal but the time came for the wedding and the holy promise had not been fulfilled, it was just like any other wedding. Both Heli and Anna were very happy for them but they wondered why their expectations had not come with this daughter. Was there to be another daughter? Was it not God's timing?

But they continued to trust in God as the years passed by, meanwhile Mary wife of Cleophas, brought forth a daughter and named her Salome. Heli and Anna watched the years go by, and it appeared that any chance of having the promised daughter grew slim.

About twenty Bc Cleophas and Mary had the firstborn son and called him Matthew (Levi). As a Levite the first-born son was taken to the temple and dedicated to God. After his time, he was taught of the Law and then the family could redeem him and pay the amount for their time there.

Then about sixteen B.C., according to the time of life, Anna brought forth her second daughter and they named her Mary. They were sure this would be the virgin woman to bring forth the Holy One, remembering that God had also blessed Sarah and Abraham in their old age and Hannah also who had been barren. Such miracles came from God.

Then about thirteen B.C., Mary, wife of Cleophas had twin sons and named them Jude, the elder and James the younger.

And the Lord blessed them again about eleven B.C. with another son and named him Simon.

And the Lord blessed them again in about eight B.C. with another son and named him Joses.

Cleophas and Mary then betrothed Salome to Zebbedee a godly man in about seven B.C., He was a fisherman who had a partner named Jonas, a fisherman with two sons; Simon (Peter) born in eighteen B.C. and Andrew born in fifteen B.C.

At about that time in six Bc, Salome, wife of Zebbedee gave birth to twin sons, James, the elder and John, the younger.

And about in five B.C., Mary, wife of Cleophas, gave birth to a girl and, wondering whether her sister Mary who was only thirteen, would be the chosen one or maybe it would be her own daughter and so gave her the name of Mary.

There were many women named Mary in this time. Strong Concordance: says that the Greek meaning of Mary is, "to be afflicted jointly, sorrow on account of someone, and be grieved." It is only fitting that Jesus would come to know so many named Mary.

There was in the days of Herod, the king of Judea, a certain priest named Zacharias, of the course of Abia: and his wife who was of the daughters of Aaron, and her name was Elisabeth.

And they were both righteous before God, walking in all the commandments and ordinances of the Lord blameless. And they had no child, because that Elisabeth had been barren, and they both were now well stricken in years.

But in two B.C., God sent an angel to Zacharias in the eighth month (October in the sacred calendar) which was the course given of the line of Abia. While he was executing the priest's office of incense before God, an Angel appeared and Zacharias was troubled as fear fell upon him. There had been no communication from God for 400 years. The angel told him, do not fear, for your prayer had been heard and thy wife Elisabeth shall bear you a son and you shall call his name John. After the angel told him all the wonderful things that would come about with this son of his, Zacharias said, "where by shall I know this? I am an old man and my wife well stricken in years."

The angel said, "I am Gabriel that stands in the presence of God; and am sent to speak to you and to show these glad tidings. And behold you will be dumb until the day that these things shall be performed, because you did not believe my words, which shall be fulfilled in their season."

When the ninth month (November) came, and his course was finished, he left for home and his wife conceived and she hid herself for five months, which was the end of March, 1B.C. She was saying *as Rachel had said,* " *God looked upon me and took away my reproach among men*".

Heli and Anna betrothed Mary to Joseph about November the ninth month of two B.C. Heli was sure and praised the Lord that he would live to see what he had believed and waited for to come to pass. He knew that he was the only line. (*Haggai 2:23 In that day, says the* LORD *of hosts, will I take thee, O Zerubbabel, my servant, the son of Shealtiel, says the* LORD, *and will make thee as a signet: for I have chosen thee, says the* LORD *of hosts.)*

And in the sixth month the angel Gabriel was sent from God to a city in Galilee, named Nazareth, to a virgin espoused to a man named Joseph, of the house of David and the virgin's name was Mary.

The angel came in unto her, and said, "Hail, thou that are highly favored, the Lord is with you: blessed are you among women." Mary was troubled by what he had said. The angel said, fear not, Mary: for you have found favor with God. And behold, you shall conceive in thy womb, and bring forth a son, you shall name him JESUS. He shall be great, and shall be called the Son of the Highest: and the Lord God shall give unto him the throne of his father David: And he will reign over the house of Jacob for ever and his of his kingdom there shall be no end. Then Mary said to the angel, "How can this be, seeing I know not a man? And the angel answered unto her, The Holy Ghost shall come upon you, and the power of the Highest shall over shadow you: therefore also that holy thing which shall be born of thee shall be called the Son of God.

And behold, thy cousin Elisabeth, she has conceived in her old age: and this is her sixth month (April or Iyar 1B.C.) who was called barren. For with God nothing is impossible.

Mary said, Behold the handmaid of the Lord; be it unto me according to your word. And the angel departed from her.

"But when the fullness of the time was come, God sent forth his Son, made of a woman, made under the law, to redeem them that were under the law, that we might receive the adoption of sons" (Galatians 4:4).

Joseph had returned from Passover and unleavened bread in Jerusalem a few days before the angel Gabriel had come to Mary. So when Mary and her parents told Joseph about what had happened, he didn't believe them but then Joseph her husband, being a just man, and not willing to make her a public example, was minded to put her away privately. Heli and Anna waited quietly but they were sure that God would show the truth to Joseph, son of Jacob, son of David; and he would believe the truth and marry the Virgin Mary.

That night an angel appeared to Joseph in a dream saying, Joseph, thou son of David, fear not to take unto thee Mary thy wife: for that which is conceived in her is of the Holy Ghost. And she shall bring forth a son, and thou shall name him Jesus: for he shall save his people from their sins. Now all this was done, that it might fulfill the prophet Isaiah's spoken of the Lord in the scriptures. "Therefore the Lord himself shall give you a sign; Behold, a virgin shall conceive, and bear a son, and shall call his name Immanuel" (Isaiah 7:14).

Then Joseph being raised from sleep did as the angel of the Lord bidden him. He arranged for the wedding in April, one BC. Shortly after the wedding, Heli passed away and was buried. They then readied Mary's house as was the Law and planned for their journey for Mary to see Elisabeth. It was almost time for first fruits and harvest and Pentecost, so it was a good time to go to Hebron and Jerusalem.

And Mary arose in those days of April and they left to hill country of Hebron, where David had reigned for seven years, in Judah. It was a long ride by donkey at about eighty-eight miles and would take about five days regardless of which trail they took. When they reached and entered the house of Zacharias she saw and saluted Elisabeth. As soon as she heard Mary's salute, the baby in Elisabeth leaped in her womb and Elisabeth were filled with the Holy Ghost, and she said, "Blessed art thou among women, and blessed is the fruit of your womb. And blessed is she that believed: for there shall be a performance of those things, which were told to her from the Lord." And Mary said, "My soul does magnify the Lord, and my spirit hath rejoiced in God my

Savior. For he has regarded the low estate of his handmaiden: for, behold, from henceforth all generations shall call me blessed. For he that is mighty has done to me great things; and holy is his name. And his mercy is on them who fear him from generation to generation."

Mary stayed with Elisabeth from about the last week in April to the second week of July when Joseph and Zacharias, who couldn't speak, returned from the harvest. It was about a three months stay and Mary was four months into her pregnancy. It was just as the very hot weather began and it was a long trip back home, but it was more downhill on the way home.

John was born to Zacharias and Elisabeth in about the first part of August 1B.C.. And it came to pass that on the eighth day they came to circumcise the child; and they called him, after his father Zacharias. But his mother answered and said, "Not so, his name is John." They brought a writing tablet to the father to write his name and he wrote, " His name is John."

And as the angel had told him, "You shall be dumb and not be able to speak, until these things shall be performed, because you did not believe my words, which shall be fulfilled in their season." And that season was now fulfilled.

He began to speak and praised the Lord. Fear came on all those that dwelt around there and wondered what kind of child this was. He was filled with the Holy Ghost and said "thou child shall be called the prophet of the Highest; for thou will go before the face of the Lord to prepare his ways; *to give knowledge of his salvation unto his people by the remission of their sins, through the tender mercy of our God*; for the dayspring from on high has visited us, to give light to those that sit in darkness and in the shadow of death, to guard our feet into the way of peace.

The child grew, waxed strong in spirit, and was in the deserts till the day of his showing unto Israel.

It came to be that in those days, in the tenth month, December (Tebeth) of One B.C., that there went out a decree from Caesar Augustus, that all the world should be taxed. And all went to be taxed, everyone into his own city. And Joseph also went up from Galilee, out of the city of Nazareth, into Judea, unto the city of David, which is called Bethlehem. Because he was of the house and linage of David, they went to be taxed with Mary his promised *wife*, being great with child. And so it was, that while they were there, the days were accomplished that she should be delivered. And she brought forth her firstborn son, and wrapped him in swaddling clothes, and laid him in a manger, because there was no room in the inn that night of December (Tebeth) the tenth month of the sacred calendar in One B.C.

God sent the angels to tell the shepherds the good tidings that, born unto them in the city of David, a Savior, which is Christ, the Lord. And this shall be a sign to you; you will find the babe wrapped in swaddling clothes, lying in a manger. And the angel saying, Glory to God in the highest and on earth peace, good will toward men. The shepherd said let us go to Bethlehem and see this thing which is come to pass, which the Lord had made known to them. They found Mary and Joseph with the babe lying in the manger and told them what the angels had told them. The next day many were returning to there own homes and Joseph found a house for them to stay, for in seven days they would go to the synagogue of Bethlehem. On the eighth day they called his name Jesus and he was circumcised.

Then they waited for her purification time of thirty-three days before they could go to the temple in Jerusalem to present him to the Lord; as it is written in the law of the Lord, every male that open the womb shall be called holy to the Lord. And to offer a sacrifice according to that which is said in the law of the Lord, a pair of turtledoves, or two young pigeons for Mary. When the time was completed they were leaving the temple when behold at that time there was a man named Simeon and that same man was just and devout, waiting for the consolation of Israel: and the Holy Ghost was upon him. And it was revealed unto him by the Holy Ghost, that he should not see death, before he had seen the Lord's Christ. He came by the Spirit into the temple when the parents brought Jesus to do for them after the custom of the law, Then he took him up and blessed him and said "Lord, now let your servant depart in peace, according to your word: For my eyes have seen thy salvation, which thou has prepared before the face of all people; a light to lighten the Gentiles, and the glory of thy people Israel."

And Mary and Joseph marveled at those things, which were spoken of him. And Simeon blessed them, and said unto Mary his mother, "Behold, this child is set for the fall and rising again of many in Israel; and for a sign which shall be spoken against; that the thoughts of many hearts may be revealed."

And there was one Anna, a prophetess, the daughter of Phanuel, of the tribe of Aser: she was of a great age, and had lived with a husband seven years from her virginity; And she was a widow of about fourscore and four years (eighty-four), which departed not from the temple, but served God with fasting and prayers night and day. And she coming in that instant gave thanks likewise unto the Lord, and spoke of him to all them that looked for redemption in Jerusalem.

Then when they had finished the customs of the Law, they returned and stayed in Bethlehem, for God had not told Joseph to leave as yet.

In the tenth month of December (Tebeth) 2 A.D., there came wise (kings) men from the east to Jerusalem saying to Herod, the king, "where is he that is born King of the Jews? For we have seen his star in the east, and are come to worship him." Herod called his priests and demanded of them where Christ would be born. "*And thou Bethlehem, in the land of Judah, art not the least among the princes of Judah: for out of thee shall come a Governor that shall rule my people Israel.*" Then Herod, when he had privately called the wise men, inquired of them *diligently* what time the star appeared. And he sent them to Bethlehem, and said, Go and search diligently for the young child; and when you have found him, bring me word again, that I may come and worship him also.

When they had heard the king, they departed; and, lo, the star, which they saw in the east, went before them, till it came and stood over where the young child was. When they saw the star, they rejoiced with exceeding great joy.

And when they were come into the house, they saw the young child with Mary his mother, and fell down, and worshipped him: and when they had opened their treasures, they presented unto him gifts; gold, and frankincense, and myrrh.

God had a reason to keep the child in Bethlehem; so the three kings would fulfill Psalms 72:10-11; the kings of Tarshish and of the isles shall bring presents: the kings of Sheba and Seba shall offer gifts. Yea, all kings shall fall down before him: all nations shall serve him.

They camped that night and being warned of God in a dream that they should not return to Herod, They departed the next day into their own country another way.

That night after they were departed, behold, the angel of the Lord appeared to Joseph in a dream, saying, "Arise, and take the young child and his mother; and flee into Egypt, and be there until I bring thee word: for Herod will seek the young child and destroy him." Then he arose, he took the young child and his mother by night, and departed into Egypt.

Then Herod when he saw that he was mocked by the wise men, he ordered his soldiers to go to Bethlehem and kill all the children two year old and younger, *according to the time that he had diligently inquired of the wise men. And so they did.*

Joseph and Mary with Jesus were there until the death of Herod that it might be fulfilled which was spoken of the Lord by the prophet Hosea, saying, "Out of Egypt have I called my son."

So when Herod was dead in 4AD, behold an angel of the Lord appeared to Joseph in a dream in Egypt, saying, Arise and take the young child and his mother, and go into the land of Israel: for they are dead which sought the young child's life. They had stayed in Egypt for two years and Jesus was about four years old. And Joseph arose, and took the young child and his mother, and came into the land of Israel. But when he heard that Archelaus did reign in Judea in the room of his father Herod, he was afraid to go thither: notwithstanding, *being warned of God* in a dream, and now they had performed all things according to the law of the Lord, he turned aside into the parts of Galilee: And he came and dwelt in the city called Nazareth: that it might be fulfilled which was spoken by the prophets, He shall be called a Nazarene.

And the child grew, and waxed strong in spirit, filled with wisdom: and the grace of God was upon him.

(I have to say that I wept over this whole part of the book. Just seeing all the planning set up by God with all the small details and such a love for all the prophets and scholars that helped to give us the King James Bible, to search out the heart of God and get to know Him. He said in Luke 11:9- 10 And I say unto you, Ask, and it shall be given you; seek, and ye shall find; knock, and it shall be opened unto you.

For every one that asks receives; and he that seeks finds; and to him that knocks it shall be opened.)

(I am so excited that 2011 was the four hundredth birthday of the King James Version of the Bible, which was finished in 1611. (After four hundred years, you can still buy them for a study Bible, How great is that?)

It is just miraculous how God's plans are always just at the right time and they always coincide with so many other people and events in perfect order. As Gabriel told Mary, "For with God nothing shall be impossible"

CHAPTER 10

WHO'S WHO

After much studying of the living word, looking for the heart of God; I have made a Who's Who of the family of Jesus and approximate Birth dates. I followed the Law as Jesus did. "I am Alpha and Omega, the beginning and the ending, said the Lord, which is, and which was, and which is to come, the Almighty." He was at the beginning of BC and the ending of BC; and He was at the beginning of AD and He will be at the ending of AD. "Who shall he teach knowledge? And whom shall he make to understand the message? Them that are weaned from the milk, and drawn from the breasts." "For precept must be upon precept, precept upon precept; line upon line, line upon line; here a little, and there a little."

I found there is a lot of, a little here and a little there. Our God is so fantastic, so big and yet He loves us beyond measure. Awesome!

Marriages:	Family Births
42 BC *Heli (Greek=lofty, same as Eli Hebrew=root is ascend) and Anna*	81 BC *Heli*
	57 BC *Anna*
42 BC *Zacharias and Elisabeth*	41 BC *Mary born to Anna*
23-22 BC *Cleophas betrothed to Mary)*	22 BC *Salome born to Mary (wife of Cleophas)*
	20 BC *Matthew born to Mary (wife of Cleophas)*
7-6 BC *Zebedee betrothed to Salome*	18 BC *Peter born son of Jonas*
2-1 BC *Joseph betrothed to Mary (Virgin)*	16 BC *Mary born to Anna (Virgin)*
14-13 AD *Peter betrothed to Mary (daughter of Mary, wife of Cleophas)*	15 BC *Andrew born son of Jonas*
	13 BC *Jude and James born to Mary (wife of Cleophas)*
	11 BC *Simon born to Mary (wife of Cleophas)*
	8 BC *Joses born to Mary (wife of Cleophas*
	6 BC *James and John born to Salome (Zebedee)*
	5 BC *Mary born to Mary (wife of Cleophas)*
	1 BC *John the Baptist*
	1 BC *Jesus born to Virgin Mary*
	15 AD *Marcus born to Mary (wife of Peter)*
Herod the Great died 4 AD	Disciple of Jesus
Jesus begins his ministry in 30 AD at about 30 years old	Barnabas (Joses) 37

The Twelve Apostles:

Sons of Jonas	Sons of Zebedee	Sons of Cleophas (Alphaeus)	Other Apostles:
Simon Peter 47	James elder 35	Matthew 49	Nathaniel/ Bartholomew– David's line Absolom.
Andrew 44	John 35	Jude/Thadddeus/ Lebbeus 42	Philip from Bethsaida
		James (younger or Less) 42	Thomas/Didymus from Galilee
		Simon the Zealot/ Canaanite 40	Judas Iscariot Son of Simon

PART THREE

GOD'S CHRIST AND THE AGE OF GRACE

CHAPTER 11

JESUS'S EARTHLY
MINISTRY

Many, many years ago God promised to come and live in the midst of his people. He fulfilled that promise by sending His Son, born an innocent child of a virgin woman born of God and would become the Lamb of God who takes away the sins of the world. He lived a perfect life without sin. At the age of about thirty he began his earthly ministry to the circumcision for the truth of God, which would fulfill all of Moses Law given unto the fathers of Israel, and that the Gentiles might glorify God for his mercy.

(Solomon prayed to God when he had finished the House of God (temple) and said, "Concerning a stranger, that is not of thy people Israel, but comes a long way for Your Name's sake. God hear from heaven, your dwelling place, and do according to all the stranger calls to you for: that all people of the earth may know Your Name, to fear you as do your people Israel; and that they may know that this house, which I have built, is called by Your Name.")

Now in twenty-nine A.D., the fifteenth year of the reign of Tiberius Caesar, Pontius Pilate being governor of Judea, and Herod Antipas being tetrarch of Galilee, and his brother Philip tetrarch of Ituraea and of the region of Trachonitis, and Lysanias the tetrarch of Abilene. Annas and Caiaphas, (Caiaphas *was appointed in 18 A.D. by a Roman prefect who preceded Pilate*) both being the high priests, the word of God came unto John, the son of Zacharias, in the wilderness.

When John, called the Baptist was about thirty years old, and he did go baptize in the wilderness, and he came into all the country about Jordan, preaching the baptism of repentance for the remission of sins. As it is written in Isaiah the prophet, *"Behold, I send my messenger before thy face, which shall prepare thy way before thee. The voice of one crying in the wilderness, Prepare ye the way of the Lord, make his paths straight."*

And John was clothed with raiment of camel's hair, and with a girdle of a skin about his loins, and he did eat locusts and wild honey. Then there went out unto him, all the land of Judea, and they of Jerusalem, and were all baptized of him in the river of Jordan, confessing their sins. And preached, saying, There cometh one mightier than I after me, the latchet of whose shoes I am not worthy to stoop down and unloose. I indeed have baptized you with water: but he shall baptize you with the Holy Ghost and fire.

And it came to pass in those days, that Jesus came from Nazareth of Galilee, unto John, to be baptized of him. But John forbade him, saying, "I have need to be baptized of thee, and come thou to me?" And Jesus answering said unto him, "suffer it to be so now: for thus it becomes us *to fulfill all righteousness.*" Then he suffered him. And Jesus, when he was baptized of John in Jordan went up straightway out of the water, he saw the heavens opened, and praying and the Spirit like a dove descending and lighting upon him: Then there came a voice from heaven, saying, "Thou art my beloved Son, in whom I am well pleased." And immediately the Spirit drove him into the wilderness, and he fasted there forty days and forty nights, he was afterward hungered, tempted by Satan, the devil of the world.

And when the tempter came to him, he said, "*If thou be the Son of God*, command that these stones be made bread."

But Jesus answered and said, "It is written, Man shall not live by bread alone, but by every word that proceeds out of the mouth of God."(De *8:3 And he humbled thee, and suffered thee to hunger, and fed thee with manna, which thou knew not, neither did thy fathers know;* that he might make thee know that man doth not live by bread only, but by every word that proceeds out of the mouth of the LORD doth man live.)

Then the devil takes him up into the holy city, and sets him on a pinnacle of the temple, and said unto him, "*If thou be the Son of God,* cast thyself down: *for it is written,* He shall give his angels charge concerning thee: and in their hands they shall bear thee up, lest at any time thou dash thy foot against a stone." (*Ps 91:11-12 For he shall give his angels charge over thee, to keep thee in all thy ways. They shall bear thee up in their hands, lest thou dash thy foot against a stone.)*

Jesus said unto him, *It is written again, Thou shall not tempt the Lord thy God (De 6:16 Ye shall not tempt the* LORD *your God, as ye tempted him in Massah.*

Again, the devil takes him up into an exceeding high mountain, and showed him all the kingdoms of the world, and the glory of them; And said unto him, "*All these things will I give thee,* if thou wilt *fall down and worship me.*"

Then said Jesus unto him, "*Get thee hence, Satan: for it is written, Thou shall worship the Lord thy God, and him only shalt thou serve. (De 6:13 Thou shalt fear the* LORD *thy God, and serve him, and shalt swear by his name.)*

Then the devil left him, and, behold, angels came and ministered unto him.

BEGINNING OF MINISTRY OF JESUS:

Now as he walked by the Sea of Galilee, he saw Simon and Andrew his brother casting a net into the sea: for they were fishers. And Jesus said unto them, Come ye after me, and I will make you to become fishers of men. And straightway they forsook their nets, and followed him. And when he had gone a little further thence, he saw James the son of Zebedee, and John his brother, who also were in the ship mending their nets. And straightway he called them: and they left their father Zebedee in the ship with the hired servants, and went after him.

After these things came Jesus and his disciples into the land of Judea; and there he tarried with them, and baptized. And John also was baptizing in Aenon near to Salim, because there was much water there: and they came, and were baptized. For John was not yet cast into prison.

Then there arose a question between some of John's disciples and the Jews about purifying.

And they came unto John, and said unto him, Rabbi, he that was with thee beyond Jordan, to whom thou barest witness, behold, the same baptized, and all men come to him. John answered and said, A man can receive nothing, except it be given. He must increase, but I must decrease.

And it came to pass in those days, which he went out into a mountain to pray, and continued all night in prayer to God. And when it was day, he called unto him his disciples: and of them he chose twelve, whom also he named apostles. And he ordained twelve, that they should be with him, and that he might send them forth to preach, he gave them power against unclean spirits, to cast them out, and to heal all manner of sickness and all manner of disease.

Now the names of the twelve apostles are these; The first, Simon, who is called Peter, and Andrew his brother; James the son of Zebedee, and John his brother; Philip, and Bartholomew

(Nathanael); Thomas (Didymus), and Matthew (Levi) the publican; James the less son of Alphaeus (Cleophas), and Lebbaeus, whose surname was Thaddaeus (Jude); Simon the Canaanite, and Judas Iscariot, who would betray him.

The stories "For every one that asks receives; and he that seeks finds; and to him that knocks it shall be opened."

Jesus and his disciples went into Capernaum; and straightway on the Sabbath day he entered into the synagogue, and taught. And they were astonished at his doctrine: for he taught them as one that had authority, and not as the scribes. And there was in their synagogue a man with an unclean spirit; and he cried out, saying, "Let us alone; what have we to do with thee, thou Jesus of Nazareth? Are you come to destroy us? I know who thou are, the Holy One of God." And Jesus rebuked him, saying, "Hold thy peace, and come out of him." And when the unclean spirit had torn him, and cried with a loud voice, he came out of him. And they were all amazed, insomuch that they questioned among themselves, saying, what thing is this? What new doctrine is this? For with authority commanded he even the unclean spirits, and they do obey him. And immediately his fame spread abroad throughout all the region round about Galilee. And forthwith, when they came out of the synagogue, they entered into the house of Simon Peter and Andrew, with James and John Zebedee. But Peter's wife's mother, Mary (wife of Cleaphas) taken with a great fever; and they told him of her. And he came and rebuked the fever and took her by the hand, and lifted her up; and immediately the fever left her, and she ministered unto them. Now when the sun was setting, all they that had any sick with divers diseases brought them unto him; and he laid his hands on every one of them, and healed them. And devils also came out of many, crying out, and saying, Thou art Christ the Son of God. And he rebuking them suffered them not to speak: for they knew that he was Christ. At even, when the sun did set, they brought unto him all that were diseased, and them that were possessed with devils. And all the city was gathered together at the door, and he healed many that were sick of divers diseases, and cast out many devils; and suffered not the devils to speak, because they knew him.

THE CERTAIN CITY AND BEHOLD
THE HEALING OF THE LEPER:

And it came to pass, when he was in a certain city, behold a man full of leprosy: who seeing Jesus fell on his face, and besought him, saying, Lord, if thou will, thou canst make me clean.

And Jesus, moved with compassion, put forth his hand, and touched him, and said unto him, I will; be thou clean. And as soon as he had spoken, immediately the leprosy departed from him, and he was cleansed. And He charged him to tell no man: but go, and show himself to the priest, and "*offer*" *for your cleansing according as Moses commanded, for a testimony unto them.*

But he went out, and began to publish it much, for he was well known, and to blaze abroad the matter, insomuch that Jesus could no more openly enter into the city, and he withdrew himself into the wilderness, and prayed, and they came to him from every quarter.

Matthew8, Mark2 and Luke5 will all tell about, Simon, the leper that Jesus had healed, is also Simon the Pharisee who had been an accountant in the temple with his son, Judas Iscariot.

Then Jesus six days before the Passover came to Bethany, where Lazarus was which had been dead, whom he raised from the dead. There they made him a supper; and Martha served: but Lazarus was one of them that sat at the table with him. Then took Mary a *pound of ointment* of spikenard, very costly, and anointed the feet of Jesus, and wiped his feet with her hair: and the house was filled with the odor of the ointment.

Then said one of his disciples, Judas Iscariot, the accountant, Simon's son, which should betray him, "Why was not this ointment sold for three hundred pence, and given to the poor?" He said this, not that he cared for the poor; but because he was a thief, and had the bag, and carried what was put in there.

Then said Jesus, "Let her alone: against the day of my burying hath she kept this. For the poor always ye have with you; but me ye have not always."

Then two days before the Passover *Simon the Pharisee (leper)* asked Jesus to have meat with him and Jesus went into the Pharisee's house, and sat down to meat.

And, behold, a woman in the city, which was a sinner, when she knew that Jesus sat at meat in the Pharisee's house, *Mary* having filled an *alabaster box of spikenard ointment*, stood at his feet behind him weeping and poured upon his head, and began to wash his feet with tears, and did wipe them with the hairs of her head, and kissed his feet, and anointed them with the ointment.

But when his disciples saw it, they had indignation, saying, "To what purpose is this waste? For this ointment might have been sold for much, and given to the poor." When Jesus understood it, he said unto them, "Why do you trouble the woman? For she hath wrought a good work upon me, for you have the poor always with you; but me you have not always. For in that she hath poured this ointment on my body, *she did it for my burial.*

Verily I say unto you, Where so ever this gospel shall be preached in the whole world, there shall also this, that this woman has done, be told for a memorial of her.

Now when the *Pharisee which had bidden him* saw it, he spoke within himself, saying, This man, if he were a prophet, would have known who and what manner of woman this is that touched him: for she is a sinner.

And Jesus answering said unto him, *Simon*, I have somewhat to say unto you. And he said, Master, say on. "There was a certain creditor, which had two debtors: the *one owed five hundred pence, and the other fifty.* And when they had nothing to pay, he frankly forgave them both. Tell me therefore, which of them will love him most?"

Simon answered and said, "I suppose that he, to whom he forgave most." And he said unto him, "Thou hast rightly judged."

And he turned to the woman, and said unto *Simon*, "See thou this woman? I entered into your house, you gave me no water for my feet: but she has washed my feet with tears, and wiped them with the hairs of her head. You gave me no kiss: but this woman since the time I came in hath not ceased to kiss my feet. My head with oil you did not anoint: but this woman hath anointed my feet with ointment. Wherefore I say unto you, Her sins, which are many, are forgiven; for she loved much: but to who little is forgiven, the same loves little." (Jesus had healed him of his leprosy but he still could only see her sins.) And Jesus said unto her, "Thy sins are forgiven." And they that sat at meat with him began to say within themselves, who is this that forgives sins also?

And Jesus said to the woman, "Thy faith hath saved thee; go in peace."

(Simon was the only leper that Jesus told to "Offer" for his cleansing those things, which Moses commanded, for a testimony unto them, because he would know what was required of him. Jesus also was telling him that those in the temple needed to be shone, and he would know what Moses commanded. The man was still called both Simon the Pharisee and Simon the Leper, who had worked in the Temple with his son, Judas, until he became a leper.)

MARVELED BY FAITH OF A GENTILE AND DISAPPOINTED WITH THE JEWISH FATHER:

Now when he had ended all his sayings in the audience of the people, he entered into Capernaum. And a certain centurion's servant, who was dear unto him, was sick, and ready to die. And when he heard of Jesus, he sent unto him the elders of the Jews, beseeching him that he would come and heal his servant. And when they came to Jesus, they besought him instantly, saying, that he was worthy for whom he should do this: For he loves our nation, and he hath built us a synagogue. And Jesus saith unto him, I will come and heal him. And when he was now not far from the house, the centurion sent friends to him, saying unto him, Lord, trouble not thyself: for I am not worthy that thou should enter under my roof: Wherefore neither thought I myself worthy to come unto thee: but say in a word, and my servant shall be healed. For I also am a man set under authority, having under me soldiers, and I say unto one, Go, and he goes; and to another, Come, and he comes and to my servant, Do this, and he does it.

When Jesus heard these things, he marveled at him, and turned him about, and said unto the people that followed him, verily I say unto you, I have not found so great faith, no, not in Israel. And I say unto you, that many shall come from the east and west, and shall sit down with Abraham, and Isaac, and Jacob, in the kingdom of heaven. But the children of the kingdom shall be cast out into outer darkness: there shall be weeping and gnashing of teeth.

And Jesus said unto the centurion, Go thy way; and as thou hast believed, so be it done unto thee. And his servant was healed in the selfsame hour.

Then Jesus came again into Cana of Galilee, where he made the water wine. And there was a certain nobleman, whose son was sick at Capernaum. When he heard that Jesus was come out of Judea into Galilee, he went unto him, and besought him that he would come down, and heal his son: for he was at the point of death. Then said Jesus unto him, "Except ye see signs and wonders, ye will not believe." (The son had already been healed by the faith of the centurion, and Jesus yesterday) The nobleman said unto him, Sir, come down or my child die. Jesus said unto him, "Go thy way; thy son lives. And the man believed the word that Jesus had spoken unto him, and he went his way. And as he was now going down, his servants met him, and told him, saying, "Thy son lives". Then enquired he of them the hour when he began to amend. And they said unto him, yesterday at the seventh hour the fever left him. So the father knew that it was at the same hour, to which Jesus said unto him, Thy son lives: and himself believed, and his whole house. This is "again" the second miracle that Jesus did, when he was come out of Judea into Galilee.

WHY DID JESUS TURN INTO NAIN?

On the way from Capernaum, it came to pass the day after, that he went into a city called Nain; and many of his disciples went with him, and much people. Now when he came nigh to the gate of the city, behold, there was a dead man carried out, the only son of his mother, and she was a widow: and much people of the city was with her. And when the Lord saw her, he had compassion on her, and said unto her, weep not. (This compassion most likely made him think of his own widow Mother who would be burying her only son soon) And he came and touched the bier: and they that bare him stood still. And he said, "Young man, I say unto thee, Arise."

And he that was dead sat up, and began to speak. And He delivered him to his mother.

And from this miracle there came a fear on all: and they glorified God, saying, that a *great prophet is risen up among us; and, That God hath visited his people. And this rumor of him went forth throughout all Judea, and throughout the entire region round about.* And the disciples of John showed him of all these things. And they came unto John, and said unto him, Rabbi, he that was with thee beyond Jordan, to whom thou barest witness, behold, the same baptized, and all men come to him.

JOHN THE BAPTIST IN PRISON:

Now when Jesus had heard that John the Baptist was cast into prison, he departed into Galilee preaching the gospel of the kingdom of God, and saying, the time is fulfilled, and the kingdom of God is at hand: repent ye, and believe the gospel.

When therefore the Lord knew how the Pharisees had heard that Jesus made and baptized more disciples than John, (Though Jesus himself baptized not, but his disciples,) And John called unto him two of his disciples sent them to Jesus, saying, Art thou he that should come? Or look we for another?

When the men were come unto him, they said, John Baptist hath sent us unto thee, saying, Art thou he that should come? Or look we for another?

And in that same hour he cured many of their infirmities and plagues, and of evil spirits; and unto many that were blind he gave sight and more. Then Jesus answering said unto them, Go your way, and tell John what things ye have seen and heard; how that the blind see, the lame walk, the lepers are cleansed, the deaf hear, the dead are raised, to the poor the gospel is preached. And blessed is he, whosoever shall not be offended in me."

And when the messengers of John were departed, he began to speak unto the people concerning John the Baptist. (John needed to hear that Jesus was doing what the scriptures had told John of the Christ's mission. His answer gave him peace and joy that his own mission had been completed and he glorified God before he died.)

JESUS SENDS OUT THE TWELVE:

Jesus sent forth the twelve, and commanded them, saying, *Go not into* the way of *the Gentiles, and* into any city of *the Samaritans you enter not:* But *go rather to the lost sheep of the house of Israel.* And as you go, preach, saying, "The kingdom of heaven is at hand."

Heal the sick, cleanse the lepers, raise the dead, and cast out devils: freely, you have received freely give. Provide neither gold, nor silver, nor brass in your purses, nor scrip for your journey, neither two coats, neither shoes, nor yet staves: for the workman is worthy of his meat. And into whatsoever city or town you shall enter, enquire who in it is worthy; and there abide till you go thence. And when you come into a house, salute it. And if the house is worthy, let your peace come upon it: but if it is not worthy, let your peace return to you. And whosoever shall not receive you, nor hear your words, when you depart out of that house or city, shake off the dust of your feet. He taught them all during his three year ministry, so when he was gone, they could carry out the plan, promised so many years ago.

John said, "This is the disciple which testifies of these things, and wrote these things: and we know that his testimony is true. And there are also *many* other things which Jesus did, the which, if they should be written every one, I suppose that even the world itself could not contain the books that should be written. Amen.

MIRACLES OF JESUS CHRIST AS THE JEWISH MESSIAH, WHICH WERE WRITTEN:

And when it was day, he departed and went into a desert place: and the people sought him, and came unto him, and stayed him that he should not depart from them. And he said unto them, I must preach the kingdom of God to other cities also: for therefore am I sent. And he preached in the synagogues of Galilee. Then was brought unto him one possessed with a devil, blind, and dumb: and *he healed him, insomuch that the blind and dumb both spoke and saw.*

And it came to pass also on another Sabbath, that he entered into the synagogue and taught: and there was a man whose *right hand was withered.* And the scribes and Pharisees watched him, whether he would heal on the Sabbath day; that they might find an accusation against him. But he knew their thoughts, and said to the man, who had the withered hand, rise up, and stand forth in the midst. And he arose and stood forth. Then said Jesus unto them, I will ask you one thing; Is it lawful on the Sabbath days to do good, or to do evil? Or to save life or to destroy it? And looking round about upon them all, he said unto the man, *Stretch forth thy hand. And he did so: and his hand was restored whole as the other.*

And Jesus said, somebody hath touched me: for I perceive that virtue is gone out of me. And the woman who had the *blood disease* had said to herself, "If I could touch the hem of his garment, I will be healed." Then when she saw that she was not hid, she came trembling, and falling down before him, she declared unto him before all the people what caused her to touch him, and how *she was healed immediately.* And he said unto her, Daughter, be of good comfort: *thy faith hath made thee whole; go in peace.*

And when Jesus departed thence, two blind men followed him, crying, and saying, Thou Son of David, have mercy on us. And when he was come into the house, the *blind men* came to him: and Jesus said unto them, *"Believe ye that I am able to do this?"* They said unto him, Yea, Lord.

Then he *touched their eyes, saying, According to your faith be it unto you. And their eyes were opened;* and Jesus straightly charged them, saying, See that no man know it. But they, when they were departed, spread abroad his fame in all that country.

And his fame went throughout all Syria: and they brought unto him all sick people that were taken with *divers diseases and torments,* and those which were *possessed with devils,* and those which were lunatic and those that had the *palsy; and he healed them.*

Now when the sun was setting, all they that had any sick with divers diseases brought them unto him; and he laid his hands on every one of them, and healed them. *And devils also came out of many,* crying out, and *saying, Thou art Christ the Son of God.* And he rebuking them suffered them not to speak: for they knew that he was Christ.

("This is so that it might be fulfilled which Isaiah the prophet, saying, "Himself took our infirmities, and bare our sicknesses.")

JESUS RAISES UP THE DEAD:

And, behold, there came a man named *Jairus*, and he was a ruler of the synagogue: and he fell down at Jesus' feet, and besought him that he would come into his house: For he had one only *daughter*, about twelve years of age, and she lay a *dying*. But as he went the people thronged him. While he yet spoke, there came one from the ruler of the synagogue's house, saying to him, Thy *daughter is dead*; trouble not the Master. But when Jesus heard it, he answered him, saying, Fear not: *believe only, and she shall be made whole*. And when he came into the house, he suffered no man to go in, save Peter, and James, and John, and the father and the mother of the maiden. And all wept, and bewailed her: but he said, *Weep not; she is not dead, but sleeps*. And they laughed him to scorn, knowing that she was dead. And he put them all out, and took her by the hand, and called, *saying, Maid, arise. And her spirit came again, and she arose* straightway: and he commanded to give her meat. And her parents were astonished: but he charged them that they should tell no man what was done.

Now a certain man was sick, named *Lazarus*, of Bethany, the town of Mary and her sister Martha. (It was that Mary which anointed the Lord with ointment, and wiped his feet with her hair, whose brother Lazarus was sick.) Therefore his sisters sent unto him, saying, Lord, behold, he whom thou loves is sick. When Jesus heard that, he said, *this sickness is not unto death, but for the glory of God, that the Son of God might be glorified* thereby. Now Jesus loved Martha, and her sister, and Lazarus. When he had heard therefore that he was sick, he abode *two days* still in the same place where he was. Then after that said he to his disciples, Let us go into Judea again.

These things said he: and after that he said unto them, our friend Lazarus sleeps; but I go, that I may awake him out of sleep. Then said his disciples, Lord, if he sleep, he shall do well. Howbeit Jesus spoke of his death: but they thought that he had spoken of taking of rest in sleep. Then said *Jesus unto them plainly; Lazarus is dead.*

Then when Jesus came, he found that he had lain in the *grave four days* already. Then Martha, as soon as she heard that Jesus was coming, went and met him: but Mary sat still in the house.

Then said Martha unto Jesus, Lord, if thou had been here, my brother had not died. But I know, that even now, whatsoever thou will ask of God, God will give it thee. Jesus said unto her, *Thy brother shall rise again.* Martha said unto him, I know that he shall rise again in the resurrection at the last day. *Jesus* said unto her, *"I am the resurrection, and the life: he that believeth in me, though he were dead, yet shall he live: And whosoever lives and believeth in me shall never die. Believe thou this"?* She said unto him, *"Yea, Lord: I believe that thou art the Christ, the Son of God, which should come into the world".* And when she had so said, she went her way, and called Mary her sister secretly, saying, "The Master is come, and calls for you." As soon as she heard that, she arose quickly, and came unto him.

Now Jesus was not yet come into the town, but was in that place where Martha met him.

When Jesus therefore saw Mary weeping, and the Jews also weeping which came with her, he groaned in the spirit, and was troubled, And said, *"Where have ye laid him?"* They said unto him, Lord, come and see. Jesus wept. Then said the Jews, Behold how he loved him! And some of them said, "Could not this man, which opened the eyes of the blind, have caused that even this man should not have died?" Jesus therefore again groaning in himself came to the grave. It was a cave, and a stone lay upon it. Jesus said, "Take ye away the stone". *Martha,* the sister of him that was dead, said unto him, *"Lord, by this time he stinks: for he has been dead four days. Jesus said unto her, "Said I not unto thee, that, if thou would believe, thou should see the glory of God?"* Then they took away the stone from the place where the dead was laid. And Jesus lifted up his eyes, and said, "Father, I thank thee that thou hast heard me. And I knew that thou heard me always: but because of the people which stand by I said it, that they may believe that thou hast sent me." And when he thus had spoken, *he cried with a loud voice, "Lazarus, come forth." And he that was dead came forth, bound hand and foot with grave clothes: and his face was bound about with a napkin.* Jesus said unto them, *"Loose him, and let him go."* Then many of the Jews, which came to Mary, and had seen the things, which Jesus did, believed on him.

THE GREAT PARABLES

And he spoke many things unto them in parables, saying, Behold, a sower went forth to sow;

And when he sowed, some *seeds* fell by *the way side*, and it was trodden down, and the fowls came and devoured them up:

When any one heard the *word* of the kingdom, and understands it not, but when they have heard, Satan cometh immediately, and takes away the *word* that was sown in their hearts.

Some *seeds* fell upon *stony places*, where they had not much earth: and forthwith they sprung up, because they had no deepness of earth: And when the sun was up, they were scorched; and because they had no root, it withered away, because it lacked moisture.

And these are they likewise which are sown on stony ground; who, when they have heard the *word*, immediately receive it with gladness; And have no root in themselves, and so endure but for a time: afterward, when affliction or persecution arises for the *word's* sake, immediately they are *offended*.

And some *seeds* fell among *thorns;* and the thorns sprung up, and choked them:

He also that received *word* among the thorns, when they have heard, go forth, and choke the *word* with cares and the *deceitfulness* riches and pleasures of this life, and the *lusts* of other things entering in and he becomes unfruitful and brings *no fruit to perfection.*

But other *seeds* fell into *good ground,* and brought forth fruit, some a hundredfold, some sixtyfold, some thirtyfold.

But he that received the *word* into the good ground is he which in an honest and good heart, having *heard* the *word,* and *understands it, keeps it,* and *brings forth, fruit with patience.*

Who hath ears to hear, let him hear.

(Of all that heard the Word of God; out of four, only one took it seriously and followed Him)

Another parable he put forth unto them, saying, "The kingdom of heaven is likened unto a man which sowed *good seed* in his field: But while men slept, his *enemy* came and *sowed tares* among the wheat, and went his way. But when the blade was sprung up, and brought forth fruit, then appeared the tares also. So the servants of the householder came and said unto him, Sir, did you *not* sow good seed in thy field? From when then has it tares? He said unto them, "An enemy has done this". The servants said unto him, Will you then that we go and gather them up? But he said, "Nay; lest while you gather up the tares, you root up also the wheat with them." Let both grow together until the harvest: and in the time of harvest I will say to the reapers, "Gather you together *first the tares,* and bind them in bundles to *burn them:* but gather the *wheat* into *my barn.*" His disciples came unto him, saying, *Declare unto us the parable of the tares of the field?*

He *answered and said unto them,* "He that *sows* the *good seed* is the Son of man (*Jesus*);

The *field* is the *world*; the *good seed* are the *children of the kingdom*; but the *tares* are the *children of the wicked one*; the *enemy* that *sowed them* is the *devil*; the *harvest* is the *end of the world*; and the *reapers* are the *angels*. As therefore the *tares* are *gathered* and *burned in the fire*; *so shall it be in the end of this world.*

The *Son of man* shall send forth *his angels*, and they shall gather out of *his kingdom* all things that *offend, and them which do iniquity*; and shall *cast* them into a furnace of *fire*: there shall be *wailing and gnashing of teeth.*

Then shall the *righteous shine forth as the sun in the kingdom of their Father.*

Who hath ears to hear, let him hear.

Hear another parable: There was a certain householder, which planted a vineyard, and hedged it round about, and dug a winepress in it, and built a tower, and let it out to husbandmen, and went into a far country: And when the time of the fruit drew near, he sent his servants to the husbandmen, that they might receive the fruits of it. And the husbandmen took his servants, and beat one, and killed another, and stoned another.

Again, he sent other servants more than the first: and they did unto them likewise.

But last of all he sent unto them his son, saying, they will reverence my son.

But when the husbandmen saw the son, they said among themselves, this is the heir; come, let us kill him, and let us seize on his inheritance. And they caught him, and cast him out of the vineyard, and slew him.

Jesus asked, "When the lord therefore of the vineyard cometh, what will he do unto those husbandmen?"

They said unto him, "He will miserably destroy those wicked men, and will let out his vineyard unto other husbandmen, which shall render him the fruits in their seasons."

Jesus said unto them, "Did you never read in the scriptures, the stone which the builders rejected, the same is become the head of the corner: this is the Lord's doing, and it is marvelous in our eyes?"

Therefore say I unto you, "the kingdom of God shall be taken from you, and given to a nation bringing forth the fruits thereof; and whosoever shall fall on this stone shall be broken: but on whomsoever it shall fall, it will grind him to powder".

And when the chief priests and Pharisees had heard his parables, they perceived that he spoke of them. But when they sought to lay hands on him, they feared the multitude, because they took him for a prophet.

PHARISEES COUNCIL FOR WHAT TO DO TO JESUS:

But some of them went their ways to the Pharisees, and told them what things Jesus had done.

Then gathered the chief priests and the Pharisees a council, and said, "What do we? For this man has done many miracles. If we let him thus alone, all men will believe on him: and the Romans shall come and take away both our place and nation." And one of them, named Caiaphas, being the high priest that same year, said unto them, You know nothing at all, Nor consider that it is expedient for us, that one man should die for the people, and that the whole nation perish not.

And this spoke he not of himself: being high priest that year, *he prophesied that "Jesus should die for that nation; And not for that nation only, but that also he should gather together in one the children of God that were scattered abroad."*

Then from that day forth they took counsel together for to put him to death.

JESUS PREPARING THE APOSTLES
FOR HIS CRUCIFIXION:

Jesus spoke to his disciples before his crucifixion and said, "Let not your heart be troubled: you believe in God, believe also in me.

"In my Father's house are many mansions: if it were not so, I would have told you. I go to prepare a place for you. And *if* I go and prepare a place for you, I will come again, and receive you unto myself; that where I am, there you may be also. Jesus said unto him, I am the way, the truth, and the life: no man cometh unto the Father, but by me. If you had known me, you should have known my Father also: and from henceforth you know him, and have seen him. *Believe thou not that I am in the Father, and the Father in me? The words that I speak unto you I speak not of myself: but the Father that dwells in me, he does the works. Believe me that I am in the Father, and the Father in me: or else believe me for the very works' sake. Verily, verily, I say unto you, He that believeth on me, the works that I do shall he do also; and greater works than these shall he do; because I go unto my Father.* And whatsoever you shall ask in my name, that will I do, that the Father may be glorified in the Son. *If* you love me, keep my commandments. And I will pray the Father, and *he shall give you another Comforter,* that he may abide with you. *If* a man love me, he will keep my words: and my Father will love him, and we will come unto him, and make our abode with you forever; even the *Spirit of truth;* whom the world cannot receive, because it sees him not, neither knows him: but you know him; for he dwells *with* you, and *shall be in you. I will not leave you comfortless: I will come to you. Yet a little while, and the world sees me no more; but you see me: because I live, you shall live also.* At that day you shall know that *I am in my Father, and you in me, and I in you.* Howbeit when he, the *Spirit of truth,* is come, he will guide you into all truth: for he shall not speak of himself; but whatsoever he shall hear, that shall he speak: and he will show you things to come. *He shall glorify me:* for he shall receive of mine, and shall show it unto you. All things that the Father hath are mine: therefore said I that he shall take of mine, and *shall show it unto you. In the last day,* that great day of the feast, Jesus stood and cried, saying, *if* any man thirst, let him come unto me, and drink. He that believes on me, as the scripture has said, out of his belly shall flow rivers of living water. (But this he spoke of *the Spirit, which they that believe on him should receive: for the* Holy Ghost *was not yet given; because that Jesus was not yet glorified.*) And *because you are sons, God has sent forth the Spirit of his Son into your hearts, crying, Abba, Father. Wherefore, you art no more a servant, but a son; and if a son, then an heir of God through Christ.*

But *the Comforter,* which is *the Holy Ghost,* whom the *Father will send in my name,* he shall teach you all things, and bring all things to your remembrance, whatsoever I have said unto you.

Peace I leave with you, my peace I give unto you: not as the world gives, give I unto you. Let not your heart be troubled, neither let it be afraid. You have heard how I said unto you, I go away, and come again unto you. If you loved me, ye would rejoice, because I said, I go unto the Father: for my Father is greater than I. And now *I have told you before it come to pass, that, when it is come to pass, you might believe.*

Nevertheless I tell you the truth; It is expedient for you that I go away: for if I go not away, the *Comforter* will not come unto you; but if I depart, I will send him unto you. And when he is come, he will reprove the world of sin, and of righteousness, and of judgment:

Of sin: because they believe not on me.

Of righteousness: because I go to my Father, and ye see me no more;

Of judgment: because the prince of this world is judged.

I have yet many things to say unto you, but you cannot bear them now.

Hereafter I will not talk much with you: for the prince of this world cometh, and hath nothing in me. But that the world may know that *I love the Father*, and as the *Father gave me commandment, even so I do. If* a man loves me, he will keep my *words*: and my Father will love him, and we will come unto him, and make our abode with you forever.

EXPLANATION OF THE VINE:

I am the true vine, and my Father is the husbandman.

Every branch in me that bears not fruit he takes away: and every branch that bears fruit, he purges it, that it may bring forth more fruit.

Now you are clean through the word, which I have spoken unto you.

Abide in me, and I in you. As the branch cannot bear fruit of itself, except it abide in the vine; no more can you, except you abide in me.

I am the vine, you are the branches: He that abides in me, and I in him, the same brings forth much fruit: for without me you can do nothing.

If a man abides not in me, he is cast forth as a branch, and is withered; and men gather them, and cast them into the fire, and they are burned.

If ye abide in me, and my words abide in you, you shall ask what you will, and it shall be done unto you. Herein is my Father glorified, that ye bear much fruit; so shall ye be my disciples.

As the Father hath loved me, so have I loved you: continue you in my love.

If you keep my commandments, you shall abide in my love; even as I have kept my Father's commandments, and abide in his love.

These things have I spoken unto you, that my joy might remain in you, and that your joy might be full. *This is my commandment, that ye love one another, as I have loved you. Greater love hath no man than this; that a man lay down his life for his friends. You are my friends, if you do whatsoever I command you.*

You have not chosen me, but I have chosen you, and ordained you, that ye should go and bring forth fruit, and that your fruit should remain: that whatsoever you shall ask of the Father in my name, he may give it you. These things I command you, that you love one another.

These things have I spoken unto you in proverbs: but the time cometh, when I shall no more speak unto you in proverbs, but I shall show you plainly of the Father.

At that day you shall ask in my name: and I say not unto you, that I will pray the Father for you:

For the Father himself loves you, because you have loved me, and have believed that I came out from God. I came forth from the Father, and am come into the world: again, I leave the world, and go to the Father. Behold, the *hour comes*, yea, is now come, that *you shall be scattered*, every man to his own, and shall leave me alone: and yet I am not alone, because the Father is with me. These things I have spoken unto you, that in me you might have peace. *In the world you shall have tribulation: but be of good cheer; I have overcome the world.*

JESUS'S PRAYER TO GOD:

These words spoke Jesus, and lifted up his eyes to heaven, and said, Father, the hour is come; glorify thy Son, that thy Son also may glorify thee: As thou hast given him power over all flesh, that he should give eternal life to as many as thou hast given him. And *this is life eternal, that they might know thee the only true God, and Jesus Christ, whom thou hast sent. I have glorified thee on the earth: I have finished the work, which thou gave me to do.* And now, O Father, glorify thou me with thine own self with the glory, which I had with thee before the world was.

I have manifested thy name unto the men, which thou gave me out of the world: Yours they were, and you gave them to me; and they have kept thy word. Now they have known that all things whatsoever you have given me are of you. For I have given unto them the words which You gave me; and they have received them, and have known surely that I came out from you, and they have believed that you did send me.

I pray for them: I pray not for the world, but for them, which thou hast given me; for they are thine. And all mine are thine, and thine are mine; and I am glorified in them.

And now I am no more in the world, but these are in the world, and I come to you. Holy Father, keep through thine own name those whom you have given me, that they may be one, as we are. And for their sakes I sanctify myself, that they also might be sanctified through the truth.

I neither pray for these alone, but for them also which shall believe on me through their word, that they all may be one; as you, Father, art in me, and I in you, that they also may be one in us: that the world may believe that thou hast sent me.

And the *glory*, which *you gave me, I have given them;* that they may be one, even as we are one: I in them, and thou in me, that they may be made perfect in one; and that the world may know that you have sent me, and have loved them, as you have loved me.

Father, I will that they also, whom you hast given me, be with me where I am; that they may behold my glory, which thou hast given me: for thou loved me before the foundation of the world. O righteous Father, the world has not known thee: but I have known thee, and these have known that thou hast sent me. And I have declared unto them thy name, and will declare it: that the love wherewith thou hast loved me may be in them, and I in them.

Then Jesus said unto them, all of you shall be offended because of me this night: for it is written, I will smite the shepherd, and the sheep of the flock shall be scattered abroad.

But after I am risen again, I will go before you into Galilee.

Peter answered and said unto him, though all men shall be offended because of thee, yet will I never be offended. Jesus said unto him, Verily I say unto thee, that this night, *before the cock crows,* you shall *deny me three times.* Peter said unto him, though I should die with thee, yet will I not deny thee. Likewise also said all the disciples.

When Jesus had spoken these words; he went forth with his disciples over the brook Cedron, where was garden Gethsemane, into which he entered, and his disciples. Then about midnight Judas, the Apostle of Jesus that betrayed him, having received a band of men and officers from the chief priests and Pharisees, came thither with lanterns and torches and weapons.

Jesus therefore, knowing all things that should come upon him, went forth, and said unto them, whom seek ye?

They answered him, Jesus of Nazareth. Jesus said unto them, I am he. And Judas also, which betrayed him, *stood with them.* As soon then as he had said unto them, " I am he", they went backward, and fell to the ground. (Showing them that he is giving his life in love, they are not taking it from him.)

Then he asked them again, whom seek ye? And they said, Jesus of Nazareth.

Jesus answered, I have told you that I am he: if therefore you seek me, let these go their way: *That the saying might be fulfilled, which he spoke, "of them which thou gave me have I lost none."*

Then Simon Peter having a sword drew it, and smote the high priest's servant, and cut off his right ear. The servant's name was Malchus. Then said Jesus unto Peter, "Put up thy sword into the sheath: the cup which my Father hath given me, shall I not drink it?" Then the band and the captain and officers of the Jews took Jesus, and bound him, And led him away to Annas first; for he was father in law to Caiaphas, which was the high priest that same year. (Caiaphas was he, which gave counsel to the Jews that it was expedient that one man should die for the people.)

Simon Peter followed Jesus, and so did another disciple (Judas): that disciple was known unto the high priest, and went in with Jesus into the palace of the high priest. But Peter stood at the door without. Then went out that other disciple (Judas), which was known unto the high priest, and spoke unto her that kept the door, and brought in Peter. Three people thought they recognized Peter with Jesus and he denied him the *three times and the cock crew and Jesus turned to see Peter* as they took him to Caiaphas. *Peter wept and ran out.*

Now Annas had sent him bound unto Caiaphas the high priest. When the morning was come, all the chief priests and elders of the people took counsel against Jesus to put him to death:

Then they led *Jesus from Caiaphas* unto the hall of judgment: and it was early; and they *themselves went not into the judgment hall, lest they should be defiled*; but that they might eat the Passover. And when they had bound him, they led him away, and delivered him to Pontius Pilate the governor.

Then *Judas*, which had betrayed him, when he saw that Jesus was condemned, repented himself, and brought again the thirty pieces of silver to the chief priests and elders, Saying, "I have sinned in that I have betrayed the innocent blood." And they said, "What is that to us? See thou to that."

And he cast down the pieces of silver in the temple, and departed, and went and hanged himself.

(*The Son of man indeed goes, as it is written of him: but woe to that man by whom the Son of man is betrayed! good were it for that man if he had never been born.*)

Then said Pilate unto them, "You take him, and judge him according to your Law". The Jews then said unto him, "It is not lawful for us to put any man to death": That the saying of Jesus might be fulfilled, which he spoke, signifying what death he should die.

Then Pilate entered into the judgment hall again, and called Jesus, and said unto him, "Art thou the King of the Jews?" Jesus answered him, "Say thou this thing of thyself, or did others tell it thee of me?"

Pilate answered, "Am I a Jew? Thy own nation and the chief priests have delivered thee unto me: what have you done?"

Jesus answered, "My kingdom is not of this world: if my kingdom were of this world, then would my servants fight, that I should *not be delivered to the Jews*: but now is my kingdom not from hence." Pilate therefore said to him, "Are you a king then?" Jesus answered; "You say that I am a king. *To this end was I born*, and for this *cause* I came into the world, that I should bear witness unto the *truth*. Everyone that is *in the truth* hears my voice."

Pilate said, "*What is truth*?" Then he went out unto them, and said, "What accusation bring ye against this man?" They answered and said unto him, "If he were not a malefactor, we would not have delivered him up unto thee." Pilate said, "He is from Galilee take him to Herod."

Now the same day Pilate and Herod were made friends together: for before they were at enmity between themselves. And Pilate, when he had called together the chief priests and the rulers and the people. Said unto them, "You have brought this man unto me, as one that perverted the people: and, behold, I, having examined him before you, have found *no fault in this man* touching those things whereof you accuse him: No, *nor did Herod*: for I sent you to him; and, lo, nothing worthy of death is done unto him." "*I will therefore chastise him, and release him*". After that the Romans let the Jews choose which to set free, a murderer or He that is called the Christ. But the chief priests and elders persuaded the multitude that they should ask for Barabbas, and destroy Jesus. They cried louder for him to be crucified. When *Pilate* saw that he could prevail nothing, but rather a tumult was made, he took water, and washed his hands before the multitude, saying, *"I am innocent of the blood of this just person: see you to it."* Then answered all the people, and said, *"His blood be on us, and on our children."*

The Romans had scourged him and beat him so badly; he needed help to carry the cross to be crucified. A man Simon the Cyrenian, who passed by, coming from the country and they laid the cross on him, that he might bear it after Jesus to Golgotha.

And when they were come unto a place called Golgotha, that is to say, a place of a skull,

They gave him vinegar to drink mingled with gall: and when he had tasted thereof, *he would not drink.* And they crucified him, and parted his garments, casting lots: that it might be fulfilled which was spoken by the prophet, *"They parted my garments among them, and upon my vesture did they cast lots."*

"Father, forgive them for they know not what they do." Their sins have been forgiven. The thief on the other cross, who had said that Jesus was innocent, asked him to remember him in his kingdom. Jesus said to him: *"verily I say unto you, today shall you be with me in paradise."*

Then he saw his mother and John (the Apostle that Jesus loved) and said: *"Woman, behold your son,* then turned to the disciple John and said: *"behold thy mother"* From that hour that disciple took her unto his own home.

Then knowing that all things were now accomplished, he turned to *last scripture* so the curse would be fulfilled, he said: *"I thirst."* And straightway one of them ran, and took a sponge, and filled it with vinegar, and put it on a reed, and gave him to drink. When *he received the sour grape vinegar* on hyssop, in truth he had taken the *generational curse* into himself on the cross. (The generation curse (Ezekiel 18:1-4 The word of the LORD came unto me again, saying, "What do you mean, that you use this proverb concerning the land of Israel, saying, The fathers have eaten sour grapes, and the children's teeth are set on edge? As I live, said the Lord GOD, you shall not have occasion any more to use this proverb in Israel.

Jeremiah 31:28-30 And it shall come to pass, that like as I have watched over them, to pluck up, and to break down, and to throw down, and to destroy, and to afflict; so will I watch over them, to build, and to plant, said the LORD. In those days they shall say no more, the fathers have eaten a sour grape, and the children's teeth are set on edge.

But every one shall die for his own iniquity: every man that eats the sour grape, his teeth shall be set on edge.*) And he said, *"It is finished."*

Now from the sixth hour there was darkness over all the land unto the ninth hour.

And about the ninth hour Jesus cried with a loud voice, saying, *"My God, My God, why have you forsaken me?"* (His Holy Father could not look at all the sins and curses that Jesus took to himself on the cross, so He turned away till the innocent blood was on the mercy seat and God accepted the sacrifice.)

And his last words were, *"Father, into thy hands I commend my spirit"* and having said that he gave up the ghost. He had died and was quickly buried in the tomb because of Passover.

In three days he was raised from the dead and for forty days was seen by the apostles and about five hundred people before *ascending up into heaven* and sat down at the right hand of his Father. (All of the Law of Moses concerning Jesus was accomplished).

Until the day in which he was taken up, after that he through the Holy Ghost had given commandments unto the apostles whom he had chosen: to whom also he showed himself alive after his passion by many infallible proofs, being seen of them forty days, and speaking of the things pertaining to the kingdom of God: and, being assembled together with them, commanded them that they should not depart from Jerusalem, but wait for the promise of the Father, which you have heard of me. For John truly baptized with water; but you shall be baptized with the Holy Ghost not many days hence. "And you shall receive power, after that the Holy Ghost is come upon you: and you shall be witnesses unto me both in Jerusalem, and in all Judea, and in Samaria, and unto the uttermost part of the earth."

But it didn't take long for the Chief Jewish religious Priests, and Pharisees and Chief Scribes to begin to use the Temple Guards to have the followers of Jesus put in prison or killed. Even used the Civil King of the Jews to do the same by killing James son of Zebedee. But when a disciple of Christ Jesus, named Stephen who was full of the Holy Ghost and preaching Jewish history including what they had done to Christ the Messiah; the Jews violently grabbed him to stone him. Stephen looked up and saw Jesus himself stood up by the throne in heaven who showed himself to the dying Disciple. We know that Jesus was sitting at the right hand of the Father and all his work was completed when he said on the cross, *"it is finished"* and approved by God. By Jesus standing, we know that there was the beginning of another plan of God ready to begin. And it was the mystery of God that was hidden for just the time as this.

Because of the Son's great love for us, he agreed to shed his blood and die on a wooden cross to pay the price for the sins of the world. He was buried and in three days the Father raised him from the dead, never to die again. All this he did because he loved his children and wanted us all to turn back to the Most High God. Jesus took our sins to the cross and by his resurrection from the dead we could receive new life.

Who is the image of the invisible God, the *firstborn of every creature?* For by him were all things created, that are in heaven, and that are in earth, visible and invisible, whether they be thrones, or dominions, or principalities, or powers: all things were created by him, and for him: And he is before all things, and by him all things consist. And he is the head of the body, the church: who is the beginning, the *firstborn from the dead*; that in all things he might have the preeminence. For it pleased the Father that in him should all fullness dwell.

The answer is: Lord Jesus Christ, Son of God.

So after Jesus was resurrected and received his new spiritual body, Mary Magdalene, who knew him well, saw him but did not recognize him until she heard his voice.

On the way to Emmaus, Jesus joined up with Cleophas, his uncle and Peter's friend Simon a tanner, and they did not recognize him, but their eyes were holden that they should not know him. *When he took bread and blessed it. They knew it was him and immediately went back to tell the eleven. And yet when John, the disciple that Jesus loved, came first to the sepulchre, and he saw, and believed. The ten believed none of them that told them that they had seen him, and he had risen from the dead. Until Jesus appeared into the locked room they were in, then they believed.*

When seven of them went out fishing, Jesus went down to the sea to see them. John recognized his voice and words and told the others that it was Jesus. Jesus said unto them, Come and dine. And none of the disciples durst ask him, "Who art thou?" knowing that it was the Lord. Jesus then came, and took bread, and gave it to them, and fish likewise.

This is now the third time that Jesus showed himself to his disciples, after that he was raised from the dead.

We will have to wait to see what our new spiritual body looks like till he returns to take those who follow him home.

(They understood none of the new things: and this saying was hid from them since the beginning of the world, neither knew they the things, which were spoken. The Mystery would now be manifested through the Apostle Paul who was Jew and Roman born and chosen by Jesus Christ for the Age of Grace.)

CHAPTER 12

BAPTISM, BORN OF WATER AND OF SPIRIT

There are many pictures God used for spiritual water Baptisms:

1. Noah, Genesis 6:12,17-18, Hebrews 11:7,1Peter 3: 20:
   And God looked upon the earth, and, behold, it was corrupt; for all flesh had corrupted his way upon the earth. And God said unto Noah, The end of all flesh is come before me; for the earth is filled with violence through them; and, behold, I will destroy them with the earth. And, behold, I, even I, do bring a flood of waters upon the earth, to destroy all flesh, wherein is the breath of life, from under heaven; and every thing that is in the earth shall die.

   But with thee will I establish my covenant; and thou shall come into the ark, thou, and thy sons, and thy wife, and thy sons' wives with thee.

   Building the Ark was Noah's mission. The rain and waters for the flood was Gods mission to cleanse the earth of wickedness and to lift the new beginning of all mankind straight out of the cleansing water like a baptism. Noah heard the Word of God and by faith Noah, being warned of God of things not seen as yet, moved with fear, prepared an ark to the saving of his house; by the which he condemned the world, and became heir of the righteousness, which is by faith. Thus did Noah; according to all that God commanded him, so did he.

When once the longsuffering of God waited in the days of Noah while the ark was a preparing; wherein few, that is, eight souls were saved by water. The like figure whereunto even baptism does also now save us but (not the putting away of the filth of the flesh, but the answer of a good conscience toward God,) by the resurrection of Jesus Christ: who is gone into heaven, and is on the right hand of God; angels and authorities and powers being made subject unto him.

2. Moses, Exodus 2:2-3, Acts 7: 21; 23, Ex 3:9-12, Ex13: 17-18, Ex12: 50-51, Ex14: 21-22:

And the women conceived, and bare a son: and when she saw him that he was a goodly child, she hid him three months. And when she could not longer hide him, she took for him an ark of bulrushes, and daubed it with slime and with pitch, and put the child therein; and she laid it in the flags by the river's brink. And when he was cast out, Pharaoh's daughter took him up, and nourished him for her own son. (Moses was also saved by an ark in the water, but was a baby)

Moses grew up as a prince of Egypt but was a Hebrew by birth. And when he was full forty years old, it came into his heart to visit his brethren the children of Israel. Trying to help the Hebrews, they turned him in for killing an Egyptian and he ran.

Forty years later in Midian, God called Moses back to Egypt; "Now therefore, behold, the cry of the children of Israel is come unto me: and I have also seen the oppression wherewith the Egyptians oppress them. Come now therefore, and I will send thee unto Pharaoh, that thou may bring forth my people the children of Israel out of Egypt."

And Moses said unto God, "Who am I, that I should go unto Pharaoh, and that I should bring forth the children of Israel out of Egypt?"

And He said, "Certainly I will be with thee; and this shall be a token unto thee, that I have sent thee: When thou hast brought forth the people out of Egypt, you shall serve God upon this mountain."

And it came to pass, when Pharaoh had let the people go, that God led them not through the way of the land of the Philistines, although that was near; for God said, "Lest peradventure the people repent when they see war, and they return to Egypt:" Thus did all the children of Israel; as the LORD commanded Moses and Aaron, so did they.

And it came to pass the selfsame day that the LORD did bring the children of Israel out of the land of Egypt by their armies. But God led the people about, through the way of the wilderness of the Red sea: and the children of Israel went up harnessed out of the land of Egypt.

And the Lord led them out through Moses. When they came to the Red Sea at the Golf of Aqaba, Moses stretched out his hand over the sea; and the LORD caused the sea to go back by a strong east wind all that night, and made the sea dry land, and the waters were divided. And the children of Israel went into the midst of the sea upon the dry ground: and the waters were a wall unto them on their right hand, and on their left. And they came straight way through the middle of the baptism water and were saved from the Egyptians. They came from bondage to a new beginning for the Hebrews. Thus did Moses; according to all that the LORD commanded him, so did he.

3. John the Baptist, Luke 1:75-80:
    The Holy Ghost gave John's father this prophecy: "And thou, child, shall be called the prophet of the Highest: for thou shall go before the face of the Lord to prepare his ways; To give knowledge of salvation unto his people by the remission of their sins, Through the tender mercy of our God; whereby the dayspring from on high hath visited us, To give light to them that sit in darkness and in the shadow of death, to guide our feet into the way of peace. And the child grew, and waxed strong in spirit, and was in the deserts till the day of his showing unto Israel."

4. John 1:6-7:
    There was a man sent from God, whose name was John, called the Baptist. For he, the same came to bear witness of the Light that all men through Christ, might believe. And saying, Repent ye: for the kingdom of heaven is at hand.

5. Isaiah 40:3, Mark 1:4, John 1:26, Luke 3:16, Matthew 3:11:
    The voice of him that cries in the wilderness, Prepare ye the way of the LORD, make straight in the desert a highway for our God. John did baptize in the wilderness, and preach the baptism of repentance for the remission of sins. And preached, "There stands one among you, whom you don't know. There comes after me one mightier than I, the latchet of whose shoes I am not worthy to stoop down and unloose. I indeed have baptized you with water: but he shall baptize you with the Holy Ghost and fire."

6. Matthew 3:13, Luke 3: 21, John 1:29-31;5:
    Now when all the people were baptized, it came to pass, that Jesus came from Galilee to Jordan unto John, to be baptized of him. The next day John saw Jesus coming unto

him, and said, "Behold the Lamb of God, which takes away the sin of the world. John bare witness of him, and cried, saying, "This is he of whom I spoke, He that cometh after me is preferred before me: for he was before me."

And I knew him not: but that he should be made manifest to Israel, therefore am I come baptizing with water.

(Jesus Christ, Son of God, Son of man was innocent of sin and John forbad him because he did not understand why Jesus wanted him to baptize him of repentance for the remission of sins when He had nothing to repent and he was to take away the sins of the world.)

7. Jesus Christ: Matthew 3: 14-17, Luke 3:21, Mark 1:10-11:
   But John had forbad him, saying, "I have need to be baptized of thee, and thou come to me"? And Jesus answering said unto him, "Suffer it to be so *now*: for thus it becomes us to fulfill all righteousness."Then he suffered him and when Jesus was being baptized, and praying, he then went up straightway out of the water: and, lo, the heaven was opened, and the Holy Ghost descended in a bodily shape like a dove upon him, and a voice came from heaven, which said, "Thou art my beloved Son; in thee I am well pleased."

8. Mark 1:12:
   And immediately the *Spirit drove him* into the wilderness for forty days and nights.

9. John 1: 33-36:
   Again the next day after John stood, and two of his disciples and looking upon Jesus as he walked, he said, Behold the Lamb of God! "I knew him not: but he that sent me to baptize with water, the same said unto me", "Upon whom thou shall see the Spirit descending, and remaining on him, the same is he which baptizes with the Holy Ghost."

And John said "I saw, and bare record that this is the Son of God".

10. John 3:1-12:

There was a man of the Pharisees, named Nicodemus, a ruler of the Jews.

The same came to Jesus by night, and said unto him, "Rabbi, we know that you are a teacher come from God: for no man can do these miracles that you do, except God be with him."

Jesus answered and said unto him, "Verily, verily, I say unto you, except a man be born again, he cannot see the kingdom of God."

Nicodemus said to him, "How can a man be born when he is old? Can he enter the second time into his mother's womb, and be born?"

Jesus answered, "Verily, verily, I say unto you, *except a man be born of water and of Spirit,* he cannot enter into the kingdom of God.

That which is born of the flesh is flesh; and that which is born of the Spirit is spirit. Marvel not *that I said to you, you must be born again.*" Nicodemus answered and said unto him, "How can these things be?" Jesus answered and said to him, "Are you a master of Israel, and know not these things? Verily, verily, I say unto you, we speak that we do know, and testify that we have seen; and you receive not our witness. If I have told you earthly things, and you believe not, how shall you believe, if I tell you of heavenly things?"

But now the righteousness of God without the Law is manifested, being witnessed by the Law and the prophets; Even the righteousness of God, which is by faith of Jesus Christ unto all and upon all them that believe: for there is no difference: For all have sinned, and come short of the glory of God. (Both Jews and Gentiles)

The baptism of Jesus was totally different than John's baptism of repentance for remission of sins. Jesus explains that his was of the Spirit and not earthly.

John 6:33 For the bread of God is he which cometh down from heaven, and gives life unto the world. We cannot give life to anyone; only God gives life even new life.

(This is so true even all through time; many scholars who have studied the scriptures with their own self-righteousness and earthly intelligence can not receive the spiritual things of God but yet testify what they have seen, but without His witness to the spiritual truths.)

Jesus is the Son of God (Spirit) and the Son of man (the Christ)

1. Luke 1:30-33:
   At the time of the Virgin Mary, the angel said unto her, "Fear not, Mary: for thou hast found favor with God. And, behold, thou shall conceive in thy womb, and bring forth a son, and shall call his name JESUS. He shall be great, and shall be called the Son of the Highest: and the Lord God shall give unto him the throne of his father David: And he shall reign over the house of Jacob for ever; and of his kingdom there shall be no end."

2. Luke 1:34-35:
   Then Mary said unto the angel, "How shall this be, seeing I know not a man?"

   And the angel answered and said unto her, "The Holy Ghost shall come upon you, and the power of the Highest shall overshadow you: therefore also that *holy thing* which shall be born of you shall be called the Son of God."

Now when the fullness of the time came, God sent forth his Son, made of a woman, made under the law, to redeem them that were under the law, that we (Gentiles) might receive the adoption of sons.

MISSIONS OF JESUS CHRIST:

A. To Fulfill the Law given to Moses:

Mt 5:16-18: Jesus said, "Let your light so shine before men, that they may see your good works, and glorify your Father which is in heaven." "Think not that I am come to destroy the Law, or the prophets: I am not come to destroy, but to fulfill". For verily I say unto you, "Till heaven and earth pass, one jot or one tittle shall in no wise pass from the law, till all be fulfilled". Fulfilled by the obedience of Jesus to all the Law and to the "it is finished" on the cross.

B. To Minister to the Jews:

Mt 20:28: Even as the Son of man came not to *be* ministered unto, but to minister, and to give his life a ransom for many. Fulfilled by teaching the true Law of old.

Romans 15:8: "Now I, Paul, say that Jesus Christ was a minister of the circumcision for the truth of God, to confirm the promises made unto the fathers."

C. To show us the love of God the Father and his own love for us :

John 3:16 For God so loved the world, that he gave his only begotten Son, that whosoever believeth in him should not perish, but have everlasting life.

1John 2:15: Love not the world, neither the things that are in the world. If any man loves the world, the love of the Father is not in him. Fulfilled by being like him that is good and humble.

D. To Die for the Remission of our sins:

Romans 3:23-25: "For all have sinned, and come short of the glory of God; Being justified freely by his grace through the redemption that is in Christ Jesus: Whom God hath set forth to be a propitiation through faith in his blood, to declare his righteousness for the remission of sins that are past, through the forbearance of God; Wherefore God also has highly exalted him, and has given him a name which is above every name: That at the *name of Jesus* every knee should bow, of things in heaven, and things in earth, and things under the earth; And that every tongue should confess that Jesus Christ is Lord, to the glory of God the Father. Fulfilled on the cross, his blood washed away the sins of the world, a gift for the asking.

E. To Destroy the works of the devil:

1John 3:8: He that commits sin is of the devil; for the devil sinned from the beginning. For this purpose the Son of God was manifested, that he might destroy the works of the devil, which comes to kill, steal and destroy. Fulfilled when he was risen from the dead and given dominion.

F. To reconcile man and God:

Ephesians 2:16: And that he might reconcile both unto God in one body by the cross, having slain the enmity thereby. 2 Corinthians 5:19: To wit, that God was in Christ, reconciling the world unto himself, not imputing their trespasses unto them; and hath committed unto us the word of reconciliation. Philippians 2: 6-8: Christ the Lord, who, being in the form of God, thought it not robbery to be equal with God: But made himself of no reputation, and took upon him the form of a servant, and was made in the likeness of men: And being found in fashion as a man, he humbled himself, and became obedient unto death, even the death of the cross. Fulfilled by making a way that we could follow Jesus and overcome the world with his victory.

Paul, Apostle of the Gentile's Baptism: Acts15:12-19, "Paul, a servant of Jesus Christ, called to be an apostle, separated unto the *gospel of God*, Which he had promised afore by his prophets in the holy scriptures, concerning his Son Jesus Christ our Lord, which was made of the seed of David according to the flesh; And declared to be the Son of God with power, according to the spirit of holiness, by the resurrection from the dead: By whom we have received grace and apostleship, for obedience to the faith among all nations, for his name: among whom are you also the called of Jesus Christ." Romans 1:1-6 The risen Lord Jesus Christ chose a man much like Moses, in that he was born in a Roman city and then was sent to a Hebrew City; He was both Jew and Roman. Both were chosen to lead Gods people from the darkness into the light, both went through many hardships. And both fulfilled their missions.

"Moreover, brethren, I declare unto you the gospel which I preached unto you, which also you have received, and wherein you stand; By which also you are saved, if you keep in memory what I preached unto you, unless you have believed in vain. For I delivered unto you first of all that which I also received, how that Christ died for our sins according to the scriptures; "And that he was buried, and that he rose again the third day according to the scriptures" (1 Corinthians 15:1-4)

And when there had been much disputing over Moses Law for Gentiles, the Apostle for the Jews called Peter rose up, and said unto them, "Men and brethren, you know how that a good while ago God made a choice among us, that the Gentiles by my mouth should hear the word of the gospel, and believe. And God, which knows the hearts, bare them witness, giving them the Holy Ghost, even as he did unto us; and put no difference between us and them, purifying their hearts by faith" (Acts 15:7-9). Then all the multitude kept silence, and gave audience to Barnabas and Paul, declaring what miracles and wonders God had wrought among the Gentiles by them.

And after they had held their peace, James answered, saying, "Men and brethren, hearken unto me: Simeon has declared how God at the first did visit the Gentiles, to take out of them a people for his name." Simeon said, "For mine eyes have seen thy salvation, which thou hast prepared before the face of all people; a light to lighten the Gentiles, and the glory of thy people Israel"The priest waited a long time to see his salvation in the baby Jesus (Luke 2:30-33).

"It seemed good unto us, being assembled with one accord, to send chosen men unto you with our beloved Barnabas and Paul." "Wherefore my sentence is, that we trouble not them, which from among the Gentiles are turned to God: That the residue of men might seek after the Lord, and all the Gentiles, upon whom my name is called, says the Lord, who does all these things. Known unto God are all his works from the beginning of the world"(Acts 15: 15-25).

"But contrariwise, when they saw that the was gospel of the uncircumcision committed unto Paul, as the gospel of the circumcision was unto Peter; For he that wrought effectually in Peter to the apostleship of the circumcision, the same was mighty in Paul toward the Gentiles.

And when James, Peter, and John, who seemed to be pillars, perceived the grace that was given unto Paul, they gave to him and Barnabas the right hands of fellowship; that we (Paul) should go unto the heathen, and they, 12 Apostles unto the circumcision" (Ga 2:7-10).

Only they agreed that they would remember the poor, the same which Paul also was forward to do.

For the love of Christ constrains us; because we thus judge, that if one man died for all, then we were all dead: And that Christ died for all, that they which live should henceforth not live unto themselves, but unto him that died for them, and rose again" (2 Col. 5:14; 9-11,13-14). "Paul, an apostle of Jesus Christ by the will of God, according to the promise of life which is in Christ Jesus" (2 Tim. 1:1). It is God who has saved us, and called us with an holy calling, not according to our works, but according to his own purpose and grace, which was given us in Christ Jesus before the world began, but is now made manifest by the appearing of our Savior Jesus Christ, who hath abolished death, and hath brought life and immortality to light through the gospel: Whereunto I Paul am appointed a preacher, and an apostle, and a teacher of the Gentiles" (2 Ti1:9-11). "Hold fast the form of sound words, which thou hast heard of me, in faith and love, which is in Christ Jesus. That good thing which was committed unto thee keep by the Holy Ghost, which dwells in us" (2 Ti1:13-14).

H. New Testament Baptism:
   a. And it came to pass, that, while Apollos was at Corinth, Paul having passed through the upper coasts came to Ephesus: and finding certain disciples,

   He said unto them, "have you received the Holy Ghost since you believed?" And they said unto him, "we have not so much as heard whether there be any Holy Ghost."

And he said unto them, unto what then were you baptized? And they said, Unto John's baptism. Then Paul said, "John verily baptized with the baptism of repentance, saying unto the people, that they should believe on him, which should come after him, that is, on Christ Jesus." When they heard this, they were baptized in the name of the Lord Jesus.

And when Paul had laid his hands upon them, the Holy Ghost came on them; and they spoke with tongues, and prophesied. And all the men were about twelve (Acts 19:1-7).

b. When they believed Philip preaching the things concerning the kingdom of God, and the name of Jesus Christ, they were baptized, both men and women. "Now when the apostles which were at Jerusalem heard that Samaria had received the word of God, they sent unto them Peter and John: Who, when they were come down, prayed for them, that they might receive the Holy Ghost:

(For as yet he was fallen upon none of them: only they were baptized in the name of the Lord Jesus.) Then laid they their hands on them, and they received the Holy Ghost" (Acts 8:14-17). Philip had left Jerusalem after Pentecost and before the rest of the Apostles. So he expected the Holy Ghost to fall on the Samaritans as He had done on all in the upper room. Philip was the only one doing signs and wonders in Samaria.)

c. Then Peter said unto them, Repent, and be baptized every one of you in the name of Jesus Christ for the remission of sins, and you shall receive the gift of the Holy Ghost" (Acts 2:38). "And fear came upon every soul: and many wonders and signs were done by the apostles" (Acts 2:43).

There was two baptisms in each of these incidents. The same as Jesus said to Nicodemus, "Verily, verily, I say unto you, except a man be born again, he cannot see the kingdom of God." "Verily, verily I say unto you, except a man be born of water and of the Spirit, he cannot enter into the kingdom of God."

This is only shone in Paul's Epistles for the mystery of God shows how we must die in order to be born again by faith in the operation of God and receive the new life in Jesus Christ.

I. First our decision: Sinners Prayer:
Acknowledge that we are sinners and need to repent of our sins. Then ask Jesus to be our Lord and Savior and to come into our hearts?

His First decision: Because we confessed our sins, God forgave us and our hearts are cleansed out of the unclean spirits and ready for our next decision.

There is more. We must be reborn. This is a parable that Jesus told them that followed him:

"When the unclean spirit is gone out of a man, he walks through dry places, seeking rest, and finds none. Then he says, "I will return into my house from whence I came out;" and when he is come, he finds it empty, swept, and garnished. Then he goes, and takes with himself seven other spirits more wicked than himself, and they enter in and dwell there: and the last state of that man is worse than the first. Even so shall it be also unto this wicked generation" (Luke 11:24-26, Matthew11: 43-45).

This is where we begin to learn about our second decision.

The sinner's prayer is like the John the Baptist making the way for Jesus. Their sins have been confessed and they have the remission of sins. But we can see what can happen if we leave out the work of God and the operation of God, which is what the Jews had done. They had no faith to believe in Him and go to the next step. There was no one to disciple the babes about the Messiah and they rejected him.

Today Bibles are readily available and we should be recommended to be read them.

Now this is the time we, for many years, gave a Bible and told them to read the gospel of John. It was imperative that we get to know the mutual love and relationship between Jesus and his Father. Also to see the mutual love and relationship that Jesus desires between him and us so we can know why did he choose to die for us, who knew him not. It is imperative to know the answer before we decide to love and die with Him.

We must remember that the first Adam was free from sin when he fell, and when we become free from sin with the blood of Christ, we are in the same place as the first Adam, sinless.

J. *Our Second decision: Will you die so he may live in you:* Jesus says we must be born again. So to live again we must die. Adam died spiritually and yet he lived, but in sin. We must die to our source of self rule and let God's Will give us a spirit life in Jesus Christ. There is only one God and we are not it.

"Know you not, that so many of us as were baptized *into* Jesus Christ were baptized into his death? Therefore we are buried with him by baptism into death: that like as Christ was raised up from the dead by the glory of the Father, even so we also should walk in newness of life" (Rom. 6:3-4).

"In whom also we are circumcised with the circumcision made without hands, in putting off the body of the sins of the flesh by the circumcision of Christ: Buried with him in baptism, wherein also you are raised with him; through the faith of the operation of God, who hath raised him from the dead. And you, being dead in our sins and the uncircumcision of our flesh, has he quickened together with him, having forgiven us all trespasses; Blotting out the handwriting of ordinances that was against us, which was contrary to us, and took it out of the way, nailing it to his cross. And having spoiled principalities and powers, he made a show of them openly, triumphing over them in it" (Col 2:11-15).

One of the questions that always come up is : How do people know what to do, if they have no one to teach them?

Traditions in the past have been changed with time. Whenever people learned that Jesus could take your sins away, they would after saying the "sinners prayer" You confess that you are a sinner and need a Savior. Jesus is the only Savior so you ask him to forgive you and be your savior and be your Lord. Amen. Then you were asked to call the number to get some resources on what you need to do. It was always a small booklet with the Gospel of John in the KJV.

It also said to find a good church.

There was much to learn in reading and preparing to get baptized.

One most important scripture is "For God so loved the world that he gave his only begotten Son, that whosoever believes in him *should* not perish but have everlasting life" (John 3: 16). You need to be careful with the word "should" because it has a maybe or something more to it. In fact the scripture in John 3:3 just before the "should" is "verily, verily, I said to you, except a man be born again, he cannot see the kingdom of God." And in John3.5 "verily, verily, I say unto you, except a man be born of water and of the Spirit, he cannot enter the kingdom of God".

It is then time to decide what Paul decided:

For I, Paul through the law I am dead to the law that I might live unto God.

It is a heart set that you can say that you have decided to walk with Jesus, no turning back.

And the cross before me, the world behind me, no turning back. Though none go with me, still I will follow, no turning back. You have to be sure before you go in the water to be baptized.

If you have set that in your heart God will meet you there and you will be yourself no more.

It is a born again of God, who is a Spirit that will begin with the Father, is the husbandman and Jesus is the vine and you are the branch. God's operation will put in a new heart and Spirit Jesus has a open pierced heart and you have a empty heart and God will graft them together in a nno second. He will also give you the Spirit of his Son and the Holy Ghost will quicken it all and you will come up born again a new creature in Christ. Then you can say what Paul has said and many brethren have said:

"I am crucified with Christ: nevertheless I live; yet not I, but Christ lives in me: and the life which I now live in the flesh, I live by the faith of the Son of God, who loved me, and gave himself for me" (Gal. 2:20).

Operation of God: "For by Grace are you saved through faith; and not of yourselves: it is a gift of God: not of works, lest any man should boast. For we are his workmanship, created in Christ Jesus unto good works, which God had before ordained that we should walk in them" (Eph. 2:8-10). We thank God for the grace and truth that he gave through his Son, Jesus Christ. With his faith and love we that believe all of his promises are saved from ourselves.

Because they regard not the works of the LORD, nor the operation of his hands, he shall destroy them, and not build them up (Unbelievers) Psalms 28:5.

David prayed "Create in me a clean heart, O God; and renew *a* right spirit within me. Cast me not away from thy presence; and take not thy holy spirit from me. Restore unto me the joy of thy salvation; and uphold me with thy free spirit" (Psalms 51:10-12).

Quicken me, O LORD, for thy name's sake: for thy righteousness' sake bring my soul out of trouble (Psalms 143:11).

In Psalms 119, he continually prayed many things to be quickened. I'm sure that it is not impossible that God had let David look down the corridors of time and see what events the LORD was planning for the future that Ezekiel had written.

During their Babylon bondage, God told them of his plan. The Lord said, "A new heart also will I give you, and a new spirit will I put within you: and I will take away the stony heart out of your flesh, and I will give you an heart of flesh. And I will put my spirit within you, and cause you to walk in my statutes, and you shall keep my judgments, and do them" (Ezekiel 36:26-27).

On the cross Jesus said to his Father: "Father into thy hand I commend my spirit." Lu23: 46.

"And because you are sons, God hath sent forth the Spirit of his Son into your hearts, crying, Abba, Father" (Galatians 4:6).

"We, giving thanks unto the Father, which hath made us qualify to be partakers of the inheritance of the saints in light: Who has delivered us from the power of darkness, and has translated us into the kingdom of his dear Son: In whom we have redemption through his blood, even the forgiveness of sins" (Colossians 1:12-14).

"Therefore if any man be in Christ, he is a new creature: old things are passed away; behold, all things are become new. And all things are of God, who hath reconciled us to himself by Jesus Christ, and hath given to us the ministry of reconciliation; To wit, that God was in Christ, reconciling the world unto himself, reconciliation. Now then we are ambassadors for Christ, as though God did beseech you by us: we pray you in Christ's stead, be you reconciled to God.

For he hath made him to be sin for us, who knew no sin; that we might be made the righteousness of God in him" (2 Corinthians 5:17-21).

[START] As we have therefore received Christ Jesus the Lord, so we walk *in him*: Rooted and built up *in him*, and established in the faith, as you have been taught, abounding therein with thanksgiving.

For *in Christ* dwells all the fullness of the Godhead bodily. And *we* are complete *in him*, which is the head of all principality and power.

And what agreement hath the temple of God with idols? For we are the temple of the living God; as God hath said, I will dwell in them, and walk in them; and I will be their God, and they shall be my people. Wherefore come out from among them, and be you separate, says the Lord, and touch not the unclean thing; and I will receive you, and will be a Father unto you, and you shall be my sons and daughters, says the Lord Almighty.

And Jesus is the head of the body, the church: who is the beginning, the firstborn from the dead, never to die again that in all things he might have the preeminence. For it pleased the Father that in Jesus should all fullness dwell; And, having made peace through the blood of his cross, by him to reconcile all things unto himself; by him, I say, whether they be things in earth, or things in heaven.

Parable on spiritually abiding in Christ after the baptism:

JESUS SAID, I AM THE TRUE VINE,
AND MY FATHER IS THE HUSBANDMAN.

Every branch in me that bears not fruit he takes away: and every branch that bears fruit, he purges it, that it may bring forth more fruit.

Now you are clean through the word that I have spoken unto you. Abide in me, and I in you. As the branch cannot bear fruit of itself, except it abide in the vine; no more can you, except you abide in me.

I am the vine, you are the branches: He that abides in me, and I in him, the same brings forth much fruit: for without me you can do nothing.

If a man abides not in me, he is cast forth as a branch, and is withered; and men gather them, and cast them into the fire, and they are burned.

If you abide in me, and my words abide in you, you shall ask what you will, and it shall be done unto you. Herein is my Father glorified, that you bear much fruit; so shall you be my disciples.

Can we ever understand that our own efforts will only cause failure, because it is God alone who can establish us in Christ Jesus? There can be no entire abiding in Christ without the giving up all that is of self. Can we trust in the Father for just one day at a time to keep us abiding in Jesus, and Jesus to keep us fruitful? Manna was given in the same daily portions to the Jews. In busy times the Father may have to step in to keep the connection with Jesus unbroken. The Husbandman, in love, will prune any shoot that will keep the branch (us) from bearing much fruit and the vine (Jesus Christ) will continue to flow his love to the branch (us) and it (we) will bear much fruit because it is God alone who can establish us in Christ Jesus.

Each day of faithfulness brings a blessing for the next; it makes both the trust and the surrender easier and more blessed. We should rejoice and accept the wondrous revelation of how God, in uniting us to Christ, has made Himself chargeable for our spiritual growth and fruitfulness. All hesitation should disappear and our whole nature would arise and fulfill our glorious destiny. Every Branch that is put into a vine needs a wound in both the vine and the branch; so they can be grafted together. We are to be joined together with Jesus through his death for our sins and we who brought the curse of sin and the beloved of the Father shared our curse and died our death. And so we share his blessing and receive his life. He took our cross as his own; we must take his wound as our own; we must be crucified with him. It is as we abide daily, deeply in the wounded heart of Jesus the Crucified One, that we have union and shall taste the sweetness of His love, the power of his life, the completeness of His salvation.

As we have therefore received Christ Jesus the Lord, so walk us in him: For in him dwells all the fullness of the Godhead bodily. And we are complete in him, which is the head of all principality and power.

And because we are sons, God hath sent forth the *Spirit of his Son* into our hearts, crying, Abba, Father. *On the cross Jesus said to his Father: "Father into thy hand I commend my spirit"*. Wherefore we are no more a servant, but a son and if a son, then an heir of God through Christ. For now, we are all the children of God, by faith *in Christ Jesus*.

For as many of us as have been baptized into Christ have put on Christ.

There is neither Jew nor Greek, there is neither bond nor free, there is neither male nor female: for we *are all one in Christ Jesus*. And if we are Christ's, then we are Abraham's *seed*, and heirs according to the promise. Now to Abraham and his seed were the promises made. He said not, "and to *seeds*", as of many; but as of *one*, and to thy *seed*, which is Christ. And this I say, that the covenant, that was *confirmed before of God in Christ*, the Law, which was four hundred and thirty years after, *cannot disannul*, that it should make the promise of none effect. For if the inheritance were of the law, it is no more of promise: but God gave it to Abraham by *promise*.

For as many as received him, to them he gave power to become the sons of God, even to them that believed on his name:

Which were born, not of blood, nor of the will of the flesh, nor of the will of man, *but of God.*

And Jesus came and spoke unto the disciples, saying, all power is given unto me in heaven and in earth. Go you therefore, and teach all nations, and preach the gospel to every creature, and baptize them in the name of the Father, and of the Son, and of the Holy Ghost: *He that believes and is baptized shall be saved*; but he that believes not shall be damned. And these signs shall follow them that believe; In my name shall they cast out devils; they shall speak with new tongues; They shall take up serpents; and if they drink any deadly thing, it shall not hurt them; they shall lay hands on the sick, and they shall recover.

So then after the Lord had spoken unto them, he was received up into heaven, and sat on the right hand of God. And they went forth, and preached everywhere, the Lord working with them, and confirming the word with signs following.

Lo, I am with you always, even unto the end of the world. Amen.

This baptism was to be the fulfillment of righteousness "*For he that knew no sin, was made sin that we might have the righteousness of God in Christ*" as he said to John the Baptist when he baptized him and that which he told to Nicodemus and taught Paul. The baptism is spiritual and that which is born of the Spirit is spirit and born of God.

"But the hour comes, and now is, when the true worshippers shall worship the Father in the spirit of truth: for the Father seeks such to worship him."

"God is a Spirit: and they that worship him must worship him in Spirit and Truth." John 4:23-24

CHAPTER 13

THE AGE OF GRACE AND PAUL'S GOSPEL

Jesus Christ was the Son of Man/Son of God with innocent blood who died for our sins. He was buried and then arose from the dead on the third day; and was seen by the twelve and then the five hundred brethren at once. He then ascended up into heaven and *sat at the right hand of God*. Jesus Christ had fulfilled all the promises God had made to the fathers and prophets of Israel. (*This is the second time that God sat down after he had done a work that was so perfect that he could sit and say it is finished. The first was creation and the second is now the work of the cross was finished*).

The day that Stephen, disciple of Jesus, being filled with the Holy Ghost, preached in the temple about all the history of the children of Israel and also that Jesus was the Christ, the anointed One, the Messiah and that they had killed him. The children of Israel became angry and called him a blasphemer and dragged him out of the temple and stoned him. Stephen looked steadfastly into heaven, and saw the glory of God, and *Jesus standing on the right hand of God*, and he said, "Behold, I see the heavens opened, and the Son of man standing on the right hand of God". Then he asked the Lord, "Lay not this sin to their charge"? And he died.

Isaiah 3:13-15: The LORD stands up to plead, and stands to judge the people. The LORD will enter into judgment with the ancients of his people, and the princes thereof: for you have eaten up the vineyard; the spoil of the poor is in your houses. What do you mean that you beat my people to pieces, and grind the faces of the poor? Said the Lord GOD of hosts.

GOD'S LAST MYSTERY PLAN BEGAN:

Man lives by every Word that proceeds out of the mouth of God.

John 3:15-16: That whosoever believeth in him *should not perish*, but have eternal life.

God so loved the world that he gave his only begotten Son that whosoever believes in him *should not perish*, but have everlasting life.

Do we not know what his only begotten Son was given to do? It was no simple task to pay for all of our sins; he died for us so that we may know his Father by believing in Jesus. We were to give our lives to Jesus and we would receive the Christ living in us. God is Spirit and we must worship him in Spirit. Yet many said they believe in Jesus but refuse to be made a brethren like Christ. It is so easy to fear that "*they should not perish*"; so change the Word to "*could not* or "*shall not*" perish and then they feel sure that they won't perish.

This is the same thing that Daniel went through and God gave him the secret so they could live.

And the *king* said unto them, "I have dreamed a *dream, and my spirit was troubled to know the dream*". And the decree went forth that the *wise men should be slain*; and *they sought Daniel and his fellows to be slain*. Then Daniel went in, and desired of the king that he would give him time, and that he would show the king the interpretation. Then Daniel went to his house, and made the thing known to Hananiah, Mishael, and Azariah, his companions: that *they would desire mercies of the God of heaven* concerning this *secret*; that Daniel and his fellows "*should not perish*" with the rest of the wise men of Babylon. Then was the *secret revealed* unto Daniel in a *night vision. Then Daniel blessed the God of heaven.* From Daniel 2:3,13,16-19.

Had they not trusted in God, no secret would be given to Daniel and his companions and they "*could have perished*" So think it over? God wrote the Word; "*should*" to make you question of why he said *should* because it is *not an absolute.* It is more like "*may not perish.*"

We also must wait for God to reveal his secret to us when we believe in his begotten Son.

JESUS CHRIST CHOSE HIS OWN APOSTLE FOR THE GOSPEL OF GOD:

Romans 1:1- 7: Paul, a servant of Jesus Christ, called to be an apostle, separated unto the gospel of God, which he had promised afore by his prophets in the holy scriptures, concerning his Son Jesus Christ our Lord, which was made of the seed of David according to the flesh; And declared to be the Son of God with power, according to the spirit of holiness, by the resurrection from the dead: By whom we have received grace and apostleship, for obedience to the faith among all nations, for his name: Among whom are you also the called of Jesus Christ: To all that be in Rome, beloved of God, called to be saints: Grace to you and peace from God our Father, and the Lord Jesus Christ.

A young man named Saul of Tarsus who was born with a duel citizenship, Jew, Tribe of Benjamin, and Roman. At fourteen, was sent by his father from Tarsus to Jerusalem to study the Law under a Pharisee named Gamaliel, a doctor of the Jewish law. When he finished his studies, and was highly educated in the Jewish Law and the Roman culture, but he was too young for the priesthood and no desire to return to Tarsus, so he became a temple guard. And he stood consenting to the stoning of Stephen but *the way* Stephen *died* pricked his heart and he began to made havoc with others who believed that Jesus was the Messiah, the Son of God. After the stoning of Stephen, he persecuted the followers of Jesus, believing he was doing it for the God of Israel. When Saul's persecutions began they scattered everywhere out of Jerusalem. Saul was breathing out threats and slaughter against the disciples of the Lord until Jerusalem had none left that would speak out. The only ones left in Jerusalem were the apostles secretly waiting for Jesus to "quickly" return. Many of the church had scattered to Damascus which began to grow in number and Saul, the temple guard, went to the high priest for letters to the Damascus synagogues to search them out and if he found any there, he would bring them back to Jerusalem (Acts9: 1-21)

Saul of Tarsus was very well known and feared in the known Roman world Until: This man would become a crucial player in the plan of the God of Israel.

God's plan had been to bring all his children together in Christ Jesus; but the Jews had rejected Jesus. God would now reveal his mystery that was hidden until this time. God would go through the Gentiles to build the church that he had planned for the Jews but they were ignorant of the Word that he spoke unto them, while he was with them that all things must be fulfilled, which were written in the law of Moses, and in the prophets, that they had killed and in the psalms, concerning God.

SALVATION CHANGES SAUL TO PAUL:

On the way to Damascus, not far from the gate, Suddenly there shined a light from heaven: and Saul fell to the earth: and heard a voice saying to him, "*Saul, Saul, why do you persecute me?*" And he said, "Who art thou, Lord?" And the Lord said, *I am Jesus whom you persecute: it is hard for thee to kick against the pricks.* And trembling and astonished he said, "Lord, what wilt thou have me to do?" And the Lord said to him, *"Arise, and go into the city, and it shall be told thee what thou must do"*. And the men, who journeyed with him stood speechless, hearing a voice, but seeing no man. And Saul arose from the earth; and when his eyes were opened, he saw no man: but they led him by the hand, and brought him into Damascus. And he was three days without sight, and neither did eat nor drink.

And there was a certain disciple at Damascus, named Ananias; and to him said the Lord in a vision, Ananias. And he said, "Behold, I am here, Lord," "Arise, and go into the street which is called Straight, and enquire in the house of Judas for one called Saul of Tarsus: for, behold, he prays and has seen in a vision a man named Ananias putting his hand on him, that he might receive his sight." Then Ananias answered, "Lord, I have heard by many of this man, how much evil he hath done to thy saints at Jerusalem: And here he hath authority from the chief priests to bind all that call on thy name". But *the Lord said unto him, "Go thy way: for he is a chosen vessel unto me, to bear my name before the Gentiles, and kings, and the children of Israel: For I will show him how great things he must suffer for my name's sake."* And Ananias went his way, and entered into the house; and putting his hands on him said, "Brother Saul, the Lord, even Jesus, that appeared unto thee in the way as thou came, has sent me, that thou might *receive thy sight, and be filled with the Holy Ghost."* And immediately there fell from his eyes, as it had been scales: and *he received sight forthwith, and arose, and was baptized.* And when he had received meat, he was strengthened. Then was Saul certain days with the disciples at Damascus. he preached Christ in the synagogues, that he is the Son of God. But all that heard him were amazed, and said; is not this he that destroyed them that called upon his name in Jerusalem and came here for the same intent?

He then ran to Arabia and spent three years with Lord Jesus Christ in the wilderness and was taught all the scriptures written concerning the Messiah and what his dispensation of the mystery plan would be. But when it pleased God, who separated me from my mother's womb, and called me by his grace, *to reveal his Son in me*, that I might preach him among the heathen; immediately I conferred not with flesh and blood: Neither went I up to Jerusalem to them which were apostles before me; but I went into Arabia, and returned again unto Damascus.

Then after three years I went up to Jerusalem to see Peter, and abode with him fifteen days Gal 1:11- 12: But I certify you, brethren that the gospel that was preached of me is not after man. For I neither received it from man, neither was I taught it, but by the revelation of Jesus Christ. Rom 1:1-6: I Paul, a servant of Jesus Christ, called to be an apostle, separated unto the gospel of God. Concerning his Son Jesus Christ our Lord, which was made of the seed of David according to the flesh; And declared to be the Son of God with power, according to the spirit of holiness, by the resurrection from the dead: By whom we have received grace and apostleship, for obedience to the faith among all nations, for his name: among whom are you also the called of Jesus Christ.

This is the New Testament in Christ's blood that was shed for many for the remission of sins and all his work before and during and after the cross, which is now:

THE AGE OF THE GRACE OF GOD.

WHAT WAS ADAM LIKE BEFORE THE FALL?

If we look at Adam at the beginning of man, it may be easier to understand the Mystery told to Paul by the Son of God. He told Paul all that he needed to do and He would be with him.

God *created man* out of the earth and breathed into his nostrils the breath of life, which filled his spirit with attributes of God, and man became *a living soul*. He also gave them, each their own *will* so they could choose God and do right. We know that *they walked in the spirit* because they could not see they were naked because *they walked in the light* (no darkness). They had been *obedient to God's* one commandment. They *walked* in the garden *with the* LORD *GOD*, but all changed when they disobeyed. They were *spiritually dead* and saw their nakedness because they were no longer in the light of God and no longer in the Garden and his blood was defiled for all mankind and they lived *in a new world of sin and death under the bondage of evil.*

SO HOW IS FIRST ADAM BEFORE THE FALL, DIFFERENT FROM WHAT GOD DESIRES FOR US TODAY?

"The Holy Ghost shall come upon thee, and the power of the Highest shall overshadow thee: therefore also that *holy thing* which shall be born of thee *shall be called the Son of God.*"

The Angel, Gabriel spoke this over the Virgin Mary for the birth of Jesus the Christ, who was born with innocent blood because God gave him spiritual life and a human seed. After the fall of Adam, we all have tainted blood and are only human and our spirit dead in sin.

Jesus came to make us to be like him and better than the first Adam (before the fall). What He had done with the first Adam, and then sent his Son to redeem us from all sin. We can then again choose the will of God and stop being our own god under Satan. So let us see how God is going to work this, in this time of grace and faith for the Gentiles first.

PAUL AND THE MYSTERY TRANSFER FROM THE JEWS TO THE GENTILES:

Romans 11:21-36 says, For I would not, brethren, that you should be ignorant of this mystery, lest you should be wise in your own conceits; that *blindness in part is happened to Israel,* until the *fullness of the Gentiles* be come in. For if God spared not the natural branches, take heed lest he also spare not thee. Behold therefore the goodness and severity of God: on them which fell, severity; but toward thee, goodness, if thou continue in his goodness: otherwise thou also shall be cut off. And they also, if they still not abide in unbelief, shall be grafted in: for God is able to graft them in again. For if you were cut out of the olive tree which is wild by nature, and were grafted contrary to nature into a good olive tree: how much more shall these, which be the natural branches, be grafted into their own olive tree?

And so all Israel shall be saved: as it is written, There shall come out of Sion, the Deliverer, and shall turn away ungodliness from Jacob: For this is my covenant unto them, when I shall take away their sins. (Second Coming of the Son of Man)

As concerning the Paul's (Saul's Roman name) *Gospel of Jesus Christ*, the Jews are *enemies for your sakes*: but as touching the election (Jewish believers of the Messiah), they are beloved for the fathers' sakes. For the gifts and calling of God are without repentance.

But as you in times past have not believed God, yet have now obtained mercy through *their unbelief*: Even so have these also now not believed, that through *your mercy they also may obtain mercy*.

For God hath concluded them *all* in *unbelief*, that *he might have mercy upon all*.

Romans 9:30-33 says, What shall we say then? That the Gentiles, which followed not after righteousness, have attained to righteousness, even the righteousness which is of faith. But Israel, which followed after the law of righteousness, hath not attained to the law of righteousness. Wherefore? Because they sought it not by faith, but as it were by the works of the law. For they stumbled at that stumbling stone; as it is written, Behold, I lay in Sion a stumbling stone and rock of offence: and whosoever believeth on him shall not be ashamed.

O the depth of the riches both of the wisdom and knowledge of God! How unsearchable are his judgments, and his ways past finding out! For who has known the mind of the Lord? Or who hath been his counselor? Or who hath first given to him, and it shall be recompensed unto him again? *For of him, and through him, and to him, are all things: to whom be glory forever* (Romans 11: 33-36).

THE GOSPEL OF JESUS CHRIST:

Given to Paul For all have sinned, and come short of the glory of God (Rom 3: 23). We have turned every one to his own way. But God commended his love toward us, in that, while we were yet sinners, Christ died for us. I Co15:3 states, For I delivered unto you first of all that which I also received, how that *Christ died* for our sins according to the scriptures; and that he *was buried*, and that he *rose again the third day* according to the scriptures: Much more then, being now justified by his blood, we shall be saved from wrath through him. For if, when we were enemies, we were *reconciled to God by the death of his Son*, much more, being reconciled, we shall be saved by his life.

I have researched through the Bible and have brought forward all those scriptures that are needed to learn about the mystery and the new creature. Enough to safely wait for our Lord Jesus Christ when you finish.

Gospel of Jesus Christ advances into the Mystery of God:

God's gifts begin when we have a new heart and the Spirit of Christ. Once we have been enlightened, there is no turning back, we have been established, anointed and sealed by God.

That the God of our Lord Jesus Christ, the Father of glory, may give unto you the spirit of wisdom and revelation in the knowledge of him: The eyes of your understanding being *enlightened*; that you may know what is the hope of his calling, and what the riches of the glory of his inheritance in the *saints*,

And what is the exceeding greatness of his power to us-ward who believe, according to the working of his mighty power, Which he wrought in Christ, when he raised him from the dead, and set him at his own right hand in the heavenly places, far above all principality, and power, and might, and dominion, and every name that is named, not only in this world, but also in that which is to come: And hath put all things under his feet, and gave him to be the head over all things to the church, which is *his body*, the fullness of him that fills all in all. After the resurrection of Christ by Father God, the Lord Jesus Christ was given all this authority (Eph 1:17-23).

Giving thanks unto the Father, which hath made us meet to be partakers of the inheritance of the *saints* in the *light*: Who *hath delivered us from the power of darkness*, and hath *translated us into the kingdom of his dear Son: In whom we have redemption through his blood, even the forgiveness of sins: Who is the image of the invisible God, the firstborn of every creature: And he is the head of the body*, the church: *who is also the* beginning, the *firstborn from the dead*; that in all things he might have the preeminence (Col 1:12-15; 18.

And he that searches the hearts, knows what is the mind of the Spirit, because he makes intercession for the *saints according to the will of God*. And we know that all things work together for good to them that *love God*, to them who are the *called according to his purpose* (Rom. 8:27-28).

God has always had a plan and a purpose to bring us out of sin and the darkness, we were so long imbedded with sin, mostly rebellion. Always. We were fulfilling the desires of the flesh and of the mind and were by nature the children of wrath. That mind is against God. Now we are asked to renew our minds and turn to Christ and his mind that was given to us.

For whom he did foreknow, he also did predestinate to *be conformed to the image of his Son, that he might be the firstborn among many brethren* (Rom 8:29).

"Therefore being justified by faith, we have peace with God through our Lord Jesus Christ: by whom also we have access by faith into this grace wherein we stand, and *rejoice* in *hope of the glory of God*. Paul, the Apostle of the Gentiles was to bring the Gentiles out from idol worship of darkness into the light of the grace of Jesus Christ" (Rom 5:1-2). Jesus had warned Saul that he would show him how much he must suffer for his names sake. In his past he had blood on his hands from the believers.

"And as we have borne the image of the earthy, we shall also bear the *image* of the heavenly. There is a natural body, and there is a spiritual body. And so it is written, the first man Adam was made a living soul; the last Adam was made a quickening spirit" (1 Cor. 15: 45; 49).

"Know we not, that so many of us as were baptized into Jesus Christ were baptized into his death? Therefore we are buried with him by baptism into death: that *like* as Christ was raised up from the dead by the glory of the Father; even so we also should walk in newness of life" (Rom 6:3-4).

"For if we have been planted together in the likeness of his death, we shall be also in the *likeness* of his resurrection: Knowing this, that *our old man is crucified with him, that the body of sin might be destroyed, that henceforth we should not serve sin.*" "For he that is dead is freed from sin" (Rom. 6:5-7).

"Now if we are *dead with Christ*, we believe that we shall also live with him: Knowing that *Christ* being raised from the dead dies no more; death hath no more dominion over him. For in that he died, he died unto sin once: but in that he lives, *he lives unto God*" (Rom. 6:8-10).

"*Buried with Christ in baptism, wherein also we are raised with him through the faith of the operation of God, who had raised him from the dead.*"

This is a difficult thing to put it all together and God desires us to put it all together so that we will see the victory of the mission of his

Son. We need to see, that likewise we are dead indeed to sin, but alive unto God through our Lord Jesus Christ.

"For in Christ Jesus neither circumcision avails any thing, nor uncircumcision, but a *new creature*" (Gal. 6: 15). Jesus chose Paul to carry out a mystery of God with the Gentiles. With faith, which works by love, we were quickened together with Christ, having forgiven all trespasses. The new creatures in Christ were to be the eventual completed kingdom of God.

And that he died for all, that we which live should not henceforth live unto ourselves, but unto him, which died for us and rose again" (2 Cor 5: 15). "Therefore *if any man be in Christ, he is a new creature*: old things are passed away; behold, all things are become new. And all things are of God, who hath reconciled us to himself by Jesus Christ, and hath given to us the ministry of reconciliation; To wit, that God was in Christ, reconciling the world unto himself, not imputing our trespasses unto us; and hath committed unto us the word of reconciliation" (2 Cor. 5: 17-19). For he hath made him to be sin for us, who knew no sin; that *we might be made the righteousness of God in him."* (2 Cor 5: 21). As told by Jesus to John the Baptist at his baptism and was fulfilled.

For *we are the temple of the living God*; as God hath said, "I will dwell in them, and walk in them; and I will be their God, and they shall be my people. Whosoever is *born of God does not commit sin*; for his seed remains in him: and *he cannot sin, because he is born of God* (1 John 3:9). Wherefore come out from among them, and you be separate, says the Lord, "and touch not the unclean thing; and *I will receive you, and will be a Father unto you, and you shall be my sons and daughters, says the Lord Almighty"* (2 Cor. 6: 17-18). This is usually where people really rebel and want to go back to their old life for many reasons. Some begin to want the neat things of the world, affliction or persecution come they are offended. Today is so loud and moving fast, which keeps people too busy to remember God. Busy is called" being under satins yoke" God is peace.

Giving thanks unto the Father, which hath made us meet to be partakers of the inheritance of the *saints* in *light*: who has delivered us from the power of darkness, and has translated us into the *kingdom of his dear Son*: In whom we have redemption through his blood, even the forgiveness of sins: Who is the *image of the invisible God, the firstborn of every creature*" (Col 1:12-15). "Even the *mystery* which hath been hid from ages and from generations, but now is made manifest to his *saints*: to whom *God would make known what is the riches of the glory of this mystery among the Gentiles; which is Christ in you, the hope of glory: Whom we preach, warning every man, and teaching every man in all wisdom; that we may present every man perfect in Christ Jesus*" (Col. 1: 26-28). "As we have therefore received Christ Jesus the Lord, so we walk *in him*: Rooted and built up *in him*, and established *in the faith*, as you have been taught, abounding therein with thanksgiving" (Col. 2:6-7). "For *in him* dwells all the *fullness of the Godhead bodily*. "And you are complete in him, which is the head of all principality and power" (Col. 2:9-10). "And having spoiled principalities and powers, he made a show of them openly, triumphing over them in it" (Col. 2:15). "And, having *made peace* through the blood of his cross, by him to *reconcile all things unto himself*; by him, I say, whether they be things in earth, or things in heaven" (Col.1:20).

And you, that were sometime alienated and enemies in your mind by wicked works, yet now hath he reconciled in the body of his flesh through death, to present you holy and unblameable and unreproveable in his sight: If you continue in the *faith* grounded and settled, and be not moved away from the *hope of the gospel*, which we have heard, and which was preached to *every creature which is under heaven*; whereof I Paul am made a minister" (Col 21-23).

BEGINNING OF PAUL'S JOURNEYS:

The Apostles all were told to preach to the Jews only and even told Paul that he was to go to Jews only but God had told Paul that he was the Apostle of the Gentiles. When the Gentiles began to understand that Jesus, Son of God had come to earth, they wanted to know more about him. It started in Antioch with men that came from Cyprus and Cyrene. *Possibly it was Simon the Cyrene that carried the cross of Jesus.* When they were come to Antioch, and spoke unto the Grecians, men that were preaching the Lord Jesus and a great number had believed. Barnabas saw the grace of God and was glad. Then he departed for Tarsus to get Paul to come to Antioch with him because the Grecians wanted to hear what he had to say. "Testifying both to the Jews, and also to the Greeks, repentance toward God, and faith toward our Lord Jesus Christ" (Acts 20:21).

"Whereof I am made a minister, according to the dispensation of God which is given to me for you, to fulfill the word of God" (Col. 1:25). "And it came to pass, that for a whole year they assembled themselves with the church, and taught many people. And the disciples were called Christians first in Antioch" (Acts 11:26).

"Then fourteen years after I (Paul) went up again to Jerusalem with Barnabas and took Titus with me also" (Gal. 2:1). "And that because of false brethren unawares brought in, who came in privily to spy out our liberty which we have in Christ Jesus, that they might bring us into bondage" (Gal. 2: 4). "But contrariwise, when they saw that the gospel of the uncircumcision was committed unto me, as the gospel of the circumcision was unto Peter; (For He that wrought effectually in Peter to the apostleship of the circumcision, the same was mighty in me toward the Gentiles:) and when James, Cephas, and John, who seemed to be pillars, perceived the grace that was given unto me, they gave to me and Barnabas the right hands of fellowship; that we should go unto the heathen, and they unto the circumcision" (Gal. 2: 7-9).

"Nevertheless, brethren, I have written the more boldly unto you in some sort, as putting you in mind, because of the grace that is given to me of God, that I should be the minister of Jesus Christ to the Gentiles, ministering the *gospel of God*, that the offering up of the *Gentiles might be acceptable, being sanctified by the Holy Ghost*" (Rom. 15:15-16).

"For as by one man's disobedience many were made sinners, so by the obedience of one shall many be made righteous" (Rom. 5:19). "For until the law, sin was in the world: but sin is not imputed when there is no law. Nevertheless death reigned from Adam to Moses, even over them that had not sinned after the similitude of Adam's transgression, *who is the figure of him that was to come.* That as sin hath reigned unto death, even *so might grace reign* through *righteousness unto eternal life by Jesus Christ our Lord* (Rom. 5: 13-14; 21). "Being then made free from sin, we became the servants of righteousness. For the wages of sin is death; but the gift of God is eternal life through Jesus Christ our Lord" (Rom. 6:18; 23).

"And be ye kind one to another, tenderhearted, forgiving one another, even as *God for Christ's sake has forgiven you*" (Eph. 4:32). "But without faith it is impossible to please him: for he that comes to God must believe that he is, and that he is a rewarder of them that diligently seek him (Heb. 11:6). "So then *faith cometh by hearing, and hearing by the word of God*" (Rom. 10:17).

"Now to him that is of power to establish you according to my gospel, and the preaching of Jesus Christ, according to the revelation of the mystery, which was kept secret since the world began, but now is made manifest, and by the scriptures of the prophets, according to the commandment of the everlasting God, made known to all nations for the obedience of faith" (Rom. 16:25-26). "How that by revelation he made known unto me the mystery; as I wrote afore in few words, whereby, when you read, you may understand my knowledge in the mystery of Christ which in other ages was not made known unto the sons of men, as the Spirit now reveals it unto his holy apostles and prophets; that the Gentiles should be fellow heirs, and of the same body, and partakers *of his promise in Christ by the gospel*: whereof I was made a minister, according to the *gift of the grace of God given unto me by the effectual working of his power* (Eph. 3: 3-7).

The gospel that Paul preached and they received and they stood by which they were saved, he declared unto the Gentiles that which he had received from Jesus, how that Christ died for our sins according to the scriptures; and that he was buried, and that he rose again the third day according to the scriptures: *Because the Lord Jesus sent him on his mission to bear His name before the Gentiles, and kings, and the children of Israel.*

"But we speak the wisdom of God in a mystery, even the hidden wisdom, which God ordained before the world unto our glory: Let a man so account of us, as of the ministers of Christ, and stewards of the mysteries of God" (1 Col. 2:7; 4:1).

If we continue in the faith grounded and settled, and be not moved away from the hope of the gospel, which we have heard, and which was preached to *every creature* which is under heaven; whereof I Paul am made a minister" (Col. 1:23). And He is the *head* of the body, the church: who is the beginning, the *firstborn from the dead*; that in all things He might have the preeminence. For it pleased the Father that in him should all fullness dwell" (Col. 1:18-19).

"To declare, I say, at this time his righteousness: that he might be just, and the justifier of him which believe in Jesus" (Rom. 3: 26). "Even as the testimony of Christ was confirmed in you: so that you come behind in no gift; waiting for the coming of our Lord Jesus Christ: who shall also confirm you, unto the end, *that you may be blameless in the day of our Lord Jesus Christ*" (1 Co1: 6-8).

God had created man with a free will so we could choose to live in the light ruled by God and love him as much as he loves us. But also, if we chose not to love Him or even not to believe God, we would truly spiritually die in darkness. The spiritual death is to fall from the light of God into darkness since we have the knowledge of the evil in the world of sin and death, ruled by Satan. Sin is so destructive and holds us in bondage; it is impossible to redeem His fallen people except through Jesus. There are many, many people who do not even know that they live in darkness because they were born in darkness. All people born after Adam fell into darkness were born as sinners and were in bondage to sin, if no innocent blood sacrifice was made. It is then only probable that sinners' will sin; but God cannot tolerate sin because He is holy and perfect. It is impossible for all men still living in darkness, whose consciences have been seared from all the bad choices that they made, to change by themselves. And some are still rejecting him today and the truth of what Jesus did for them; just as they did two thousand years ago.

But they have not listened to the gospel given to Paul, the Apostle and have not believed by faith that it is true that Jesus died for our sins and was buried and in three days, God raised him up.

He loves all and wants no one to perish but all to be with Him for all eternity. God had made the plan of redemption and a way to escape sin even before He created us. This is what they need to hear and believe it by faith. For God so loves us that he doesn't want any to perish.

Jesus was wounded for our transgressions, he was bruised for our iniquities: the chastisement of our peace was upon him, and with his stripes we were healed. Jesus died for our sins on the cross according to the scriptures; and that he was buried, and in three days, he rose again according to the scriptures that were written thousands of years ago. This is the gospel Paul preached. We can give thanks unto the Father, which has enabled us to be partakers of the inheritance of the *saints* in light: who has delivered us from the power of darkness, and has translated us into the kingdom of his dear Son in whom we have redemption through his blood, even the forgiveness of sins: *who is the image of the invisible God, the firstborn of every creature.* "For this is good and acceptable in the sight of God our Savior who will to have all men saved, and to come to the knowledge of the truth. For there is one God, and one mediator between God and men, the man Jesus Christ" (1 Tim. 2: 3-5). "And without controversy great is the mystery of godliness:

God was manifest in the flesh, justified in the Spirit, seen of angels, preached unto the Gentiles, believed on in the world, received up into glory" (1Tim. 3:16). "As for us, therefore being justified by faith, we have peace with God through our Lord Jesus Christ: by whom also we have access by faith into this grace wherein we stand, and rejoice in hope of the glory of God" Rom. 5: 1-2).

"For the grace of God that brings salvation has appeared to all men, teaching us that, denying ungodliness and worldly lusts, we should live soberly, righteously, and godly, in this present world; looking for that blessed hope, and the glorious appearing of the great God and our Savior Jesus Christ; who gave himself for us, that He might redeem us from all iniquity, and purify unto himself a peculiar people, zealous of good works" (Tit 2: 11-14). "Now all things are of God, who has reconciled us to Himself through Jesus Christ, and has given us the ministry of reconciliation, that is, that God was in Christ reconciling the world to Himself, not imputing their trespasses to them, and has committed to us the word of reconciliation. Therefore we are ambassadors for Christ, as though God were pleading through us: we implore you on Christ's behalf, be reconciled to God. *For He made Him who knew no sin to be sin for us, that we might become the righteousness of God* (2 Co 5:17-21). I beseech you therefore, brethren, by the mercies of God, that you *present your bodies a living sacrifice, holy, acceptable to God,*

which is your reasonable service. And do not be conformed to this world, and *be transformed by the renewing of your mind*, that you may prove what is that *good and acceptable and perfect will of God*" (Rom. 12:1-2).

"This is the good news and why the Father sent His only begotten Son to bring light into a dark world and bring us the hope of eternal life with Him through faith and grace for all believers."

THESE ARE PAUL'S TEACHINGS TO THE NEW CREATURES:

" If ye have heard of the *dispensation of the grace of God* which is given me to you-ward: *How that by revelation he made known unto me the mystery;* as I wrote afore in few words, (Whereby, when you read, you may understand my knowledge in the mystery of Christ). Which in other ages was not made known unto the sons of men, as it is now revealed unto his holy apostles and prophets by the Spirit; That the *Gentiles should be fellow heirs*, and of the same body, and partakers of his promise in Christ by the gospel: Whereof I was made a minister, according to the gift of the grace of God given unto me by the effectual working of his power. Unto me, who am less than the least of all saints, is this grace given, that I should preach among the Gentiles the unsearchable riches of Christ; And to make all men see *what is the fellowship* of the *mystery*, which *from the beginning of the world hath been hid in God*, who created all things by Jesus Christ: To the intent that now unto *the principalities and powers in heavenly places might be known by the church the manifold wisdom of God, according to the eternal purpose which he purposed in Christ Jesus our Lord: In whom we have boldness and access with confidence by the faith of him*" (Eph. 3:2-12).

"Whereof I (Paul) am made a minister, according to the dispensation of God which is given to me for you, to fulfill the word of God; Even the mystery which hath been *hid* from ages and from generations, *but now* is made *manifest to his saints*: To whom God would make known what is the *riches of the glory* of this mystery among the *Gentiles; which is Christ in you, the hope of glory:* Whom we preach, warning every man, and teaching every man in all wisdom; that *we may present every man perfect in Christ Jesus*: Whereunto I also labor, striving according to his working, which works in me mightily" (Col. 1:25-29).

Now then we are ambassadors for Christ, as though God did beseech you by us: we pray you in Christ's stead, be ye reconciled to God. For *He has made Christ to be sin for us, who knew no sin; that we might be made the righteousness of God in Christ*" (2 Cor. 5:20-21).

"Neither is there any *creature* that is *not* manifest in his sight: *but all things* are naked and opened unto the *eyes of Him* with whom we have to do." "Though the Lord be high, yet he has respect unto the lowly: but the proud he knows afar" (Ps 138:6). Seeing then that we have a Great High Priest that is passed into the heavens, Jesus the Son of God, let us hold fast our profession. For we have not an high priest which cannot be touched with the feeling of our infirmities; but was in all points tempted like as we are, yet without sin. Let us therefore come boldly unto the throne of grace that we may obtain mercy, and find grace to help in time of need" (Heb. 4:13-16).

"As you have therefore received Christ Jesus the Lord, so walk you *in him*:" "For *in him* dwells all the fullness of the Godhead bodily." "And you are complete in him, which is the head of all principality and power" (Col. 2:6; 9-15).

Knowing this, that our old man is crucified with him, that the body of sin might be destroyed, that henceforth we should not serve sin. For he that is dead is freed from sin" (Rom. 6:3). "*I am crucified with Christ: nevertheless I live; yet not I, but Christ lives in me: and the life which I now live in the flesh I live by the faith of the Son of God, who loved me, and gave himself for me*" (Gal 2: 20). "Now if we be dead with Christ, we believe that we shall also live with him: Knowing that Christ being raised from the dead dies no more; death hath no more dominion over him. For in that he died, he died unto sin once: but in that he lives, he lives unto God. Likewise reckon we also ourselves to be dead indeed unto sin, but alive unto God through Jesus Christ our Lord" (Rom. 6:3; 10-11).

"For you are all the children of God *by faith in Christ Jesus.* For as many of you as have been *baptized into Christ* have put on Christ. There is neither Jew nor Greek, there is neither bond nor free, there is neither male nor female: for we are all one in Christ Jesus. And if you be Christ's, then are you Abraham's seed, and heirs according to the promise" (Gal. 3:26-29). "*And in thy seed shall all the nations of the earth be blessed; because thou hast obeyed my voice*" (Gen. 22: 18).

"For the love of Christ constraints us; because we thus judge, that if one died for all, then were all dead": And that he died for all, that they which live should not henceforth live unto themselves, but unto him which died for them, and rose again." "Wherefore henceforth know we no man after the flesh: yea, though we have known Christ after the flesh, yet now henceforth know we him no more" (2 Co 5:14-16).

"The Spirit itself bears witness with our spirit, that we are the children of God": "And if children, then heirs; heirs of God, and joint-heirs with Christ; if so be that we suffer with him, that we may be also glorified together." "For I reckon that the sufferings of this present time are not worthy to be compared with the glory, which shall be revealed in us" (Rom. 8:16-18).

"That the God of our Lord Jesus Christ, the Father of glory, may give unto you the spirit of wisdom and revelation in the knowledge of him. The eyes of your understanding being enlightened; that ye may know what is the hope of his calling, and what the riches of the glory of his inheritance in the *saints*, And what is the exceeding greatness of his power to us-ward who believe, according to the working of his mighty power, Which he wrought in Christ, when he raised him from the dead, and set him at his own right hand in the heavenly places. Far above all principality, and power, and might, and dominion, and every name that is named, not only in this world, but also in that which is to come: and hath put all things under his feet, and gave him to be the head over all things to the church, which is his body, the fullness of him that fills all in all (Eph. 1: 17-23). I beseech you therefore, brethren, by the mercies of God, that you present your bodies a living sacrifice, holy, acceptable unto God, which is your reasonable service. And be not conformed to this world: but be ye transformed by the *renewing of your mind*, that you may *prove what is that good, and acceptable, and perfect, will of God*. For I say, through the grace given unto me, to every man that is among you, not to think of himself more highly than he ought to think; but to think soberly, according as God hath dealt to *every man the measure of faith*. For as we have *many members* in one body, and all members have not the same office: So we, being many, are *one body in Christ*, and every one members one of another" (Rom. 12:1-5).

"For the perfecting of the *saints*, for the work of the ministry, for the edifying of the body of Christ: *Till we all come in the unity of the faith, and of the knowledge of the Son of God, unto a perfect man, unto the measure of the stature of the fullness of Christ*: That we henceforth be no more children, tossed to and fro, and carried about with every wind of doctrine, by the sleight of men, and cunning craftiness, whereby they lie in wait to deceive; But speaking the truth in love, may grow up into him in all things, which is the head, even Christ: From whom the whole body fitly joined together and compacted by that which every joint supplies, according to the effectual working in the measure of every part, makes increase of the body unto the edifying of itself in love" (Eph 4:12-16).

WHY TRUE LOVE IS MOST IMPORTANT TO GOD AND TO PAUL:

We were given only two commandments that cover all the rest: to Love God and our neighbors.

"Beloved let us love one another: for love is of God; and every one that loves is born of God, and knows God. In this was manifested the love of God toward us, because that God sent his only begotten Son into the world, that we might live through him. Herein is love, not that we loved God, but that he loved us, and sent his Son to be the propitiation for our sins. Beloved, if God so loved us, we ought also to love one another. No man hath seen God at any time. If we love one another, God dwells in us, and his love is perfected in us" (1 Job 4:7; 9-12).

"But I say unto you, Love your enemies, bless them that curse you, do good to them that hate you, and pray for them which despitefully use you, and persecute you"; "That you may be the children of your Father, which is in heaven: for he makes his sun to rise on the evil and on the good, and sends rain on the just and on the unjust. Be ye therefore perfect, even as your Father, which is in heaven, is perfect" (Mal. 5:44-45; 48).

The Apostle Paul learned and taught these principles of God's Love all through his journeying in his Lord Jesus Christ:

God's true love (charity):

1. Though I speak with the tongues of men and of angels, and have not charity (*true love*), I am become as sounding brass, or a tinkling cymbal. *Settle it therefore in your hearts, not to meditate before what ye shall answer: For I will give you a mouth and wisdom, which all your adversaries shall not be able to gainsay nor resist (Luke 21:14-15).* "But I certify

you, brethren, that the gospel which was preached of me is not after man. For I neither received it of man, neither was I taught it, but by the revelation of Jesus Christ" (Gal 1:11-12).

2. And though I have the gift of prophecy, and understand all mysteries, and all knowledge; and though I have all faith, so that I could remove mountains, and have not charity, I am nothing. *This is what happened to those: "Many will say to me in that day, Lord, Lord, have we not prophesied in thy name? and in thy name have cast out devils? and in thy name done many wonderful works? And then will I profess unto them, I never knew you" (Matthew 7:22-23). "He that hath my commandments, and keeps them, he it is that loves me: and he that loves me shall be loved of my Father, and I will love him, and will manifest myself to him" (John 14:21).*

3. And though I bestow all my goods to feed the poor, and though I give my body to be burned, and have not charity, it profits me nothing. *"Therefore when you do your alms, do not sound a trumpet before you, as the hypocrites do in the synagogues and in the streets, that they may have glory from men. Verily I say unto you, they have their reward" (Matthew 6:2).*

4. Charity suffers long. *"The Lord is not slack concerning his promise, as some men count slackness; but is longsuffering to us-ward, not willing that any should perish, but that all should come to repentance" (2 Peter 3:9).* And love is kind. *"And be ye kind one to another, tenderhearted, forgiving one another, even as God for Christ's sake hath forgiven you" (Eph. 4:32).*

    Charity envies not. *"Fret not thyself because of evildoers, neither be thou envious against the workers of iniquity" (Psalms 37:1);* charity vaunts not itself *"Be not rash with thy mouth, and let not thine heart be hasty to utter any thing before God: for God is in heaven, and thou upon earth: therefore let thy words be few" (Ecc1 5:2).* Love is not puffed up *"And ye are puffed up, and have not rather mourned, that he that hath done this deed might be taken away from among you" (1 Col. 5: 2).*

5. Love does not behave itself unseemly. *"Be of good courage, and let us behave ourselves valiantly for our people, and for the cities of our God: and let the* Lord *do that which is good in his sight" (1 Col. 19:13).* Love seeks not her own: *"I can of mine own self do nothing: as I hear, I judge: and my judgment is just; because I seek not mine own will, but the will of the Father which hath sent me" (John 5:30).* Love is not easily provoked: *"And let us consider one another to provoke unto love and to good works" (Heb. 10:24).* Love thinks no evil: *"Finally, be ye all of one mind, having compassion one of another, love as brethren, be pitiful, be courteous" (1 Peter 3:8).*

6. Rejoices not in iniquity, but rejoices in the truth: *"Rejoice not when thine enemy falls, and let not thine heart be glad when he stumbles"(Pr 24:17). "I rejoiced greatly that I found of thy children walking in truth, as we have received a commandment from the Father."2Jo1:4. But Christ as a son over his own house; whose house are we, if we hold fast the confidence and the rejoicing of the hope firm unto the end" (Heb. 3:6).*

7. Love bears all things: *"Bear ye one another's burdens, and so fulfill the law of Christ" (Gal 6:2).*

8. Love believes all things: *"Jesus said unto him, If thou canst believe, all things are possible to him that believeth" (Mk 9:23).*

9. Love hopes all things: *"Now the God of hope fill you with all joy and peace in believing, that ye may abound in hope, through the power of the Holy Ghost" (Rom. 15:13).*

10. And love endures all things: *"Therefore I endure all things for the elect's sakes, that they may also obtain the salvation which is in Christ Jesus with eternal glory" (2 Tim. 2:10).*

11. Charity (love) never fails: "*For I am persuaded, that neither death, nor life, nor angels, nor principalities, nor powers, nor things present, nor things to come, Nor height, nor depth, nor any other creature, shall be able to separate us from the love of God, which is in Christ Jesus our Lord*" (Rom. 8:38-39).

But whether there be prophecies, they shall fail; whether there be tongues, they shall cease; whether there be knowledge, it shall vanish away. For we know in part, and we prophesy in part.

12. But when that which is perfect is come, *then that which is in part shall be done away.*

When I was a child, I spoke as a child, I understood as a child, I thought as a child: but when I became a man, I put away childish things.

For now we see through a glass, darkly; but then face to face: now I know in part; but then shall I know even as also I am known.

And now abides faith, hope, charity, these three; but the greatest of these is charity (true love).

(This is of this wonderful chapter on true love, which must have touched the heart of God and Paul. And it should touch the heart of many persons).

Acts 10:38 states, How God anointed Jesus of Nazareth with the Holy Ghost and with power: who went about doing good, and healing all that were oppressed of the devil; for God was with him.

Below is a statement from a blessed Albert Barnes Commentary:

(1.) That no man is a Christian who lives for himself alone; or who makes it his main business to promote his own happiness and salvation.

(2.) No man is a Christian who does not deny himself; or no one who is not willing to sacrifice: his own comfort, time, wealth, and ease, to advance the welfare of mankind.

(3.) It is this principle, which is yet to convert the world. *Long since the whole world would have been converted, had all Christians been under its influence. And when ALL Christians make it their grand object not to seek their own, but the good of others; when true charity shall occupy its appropriate place in the heart of every professed child of God, then this world will be speedily converted to the Savior. Then there will be no want of funds to spread Bibles and tracts; to sustain missionaries, or to establish colleges and schools; then there will be no want of men who shall be willing to go to any part of the earth to preach the gospel; and then there will be no want of prayer to implore the Divine mercy on a ruined and perishing world. Oh, may the time soon come when all the selfishness in the human heart shall be dissolved, and when the whole world shall be embraced in the benevolence of Christians, and the time, and talent, and wealth of the whole church shall be regarded as consecrated to God, and employed and expended under the influence of Christian love!*

Now that you have read this commentary, I can't help but believe, that you will see the desire of God's heart and his longsuffering of waiting for the Body of Christ to mirror this commentary.

We who are believers saved by grace through faith wait on the hope of the return of the Lord Jesus Christ to take us up to his home through the rapture and be with Him forever.

I am Alpha and Omega, the beginning and the ending, said the Lord, which is, and was, and which is to come, the Almighty. Re 1:8

We must be born again of God and only He can bring new life in us with his Spirit of Truth, and the Holy Ghost.

Jesus is the way, the truth and the life, (Jesus gave his *Spirit of truth* to the *Father* when he was on the cross) and the *operation of God* was given to us in the baptisms of *water* along with a new heart and the Holy Spirit. Galatians 4:4-7 But when the fullness of the time was come, God sent forth his Son, made of a woman, made under the law, to redeem them that were under the law, that we might receive the adoption of sons. And then because we are sons, *God hath sent forth the Spirit of his Son into your hearts, crying, Abba, Father*. Wherefore you are no more a servant, but a son; and if a son, then an *heir of God through Christ*.

This is the mystery, which was hid from the ages and generations, but is now made manifest to his *saints*. To whom God would make known what is the riches of the glory of this mystery among the Gentiles; which is Christ in us, the hope of glory: whom we preach, warning every man (and woman), and teaching them in all wisdom; that we may present every man and woman perfect in Christ Jesus (*Col 1:26-27*).

Whereunto I (Paul) also labor, striving according to his working, which works in me mightily. Wherefore I take you to record this day that I am pure from the blood of all men.

(No longer Saul)

Take heed therefore unto yourselves, and to all of the flock, over which the Holy Ghost has made you overseers, to feed the church of God, which he has purchased with his own blood.

And now brethren, I commend you to God and to the word of his grace, which is able to build you up, and give you an inheritance among all them that are sanctified.

I have shown you all things.

CHAPTER 14

THE SECOND CHANCE

So, if you are a reader of the last page to see how it ends, this is for you.

In the beginning God created human man and woman. They were earthly and spiritual beings that only knew "good". They walked and talked with God and worked in the Garden of Eden and He wants the same thing for us. When they disobeyed God the spiritual being died but earthly remained. All human beings have been born sinners from the day Adam and Eve fell to this end of the world. The world they had inherited from God was love, peace and goodness and they turned it into sin, defiled blood and death; that is what we inherited. But God always had a plan and picked one group of people and worked for centuries to turn them back to him by faith (believing that he is the truth) but to no avail. Surely when he sent his only begotten Son; who had innocent blood and no sin; who was ready to die and pay for the sins of whosoever believed in him.

He was born the Son of God and Son of man. He was the firstborn Creature and the hope of many brethren to follow in him. Jesus told us that we must be born- again or we will not see the kingdom of God. To be born again, a person must die and be born again.

And when he had called the people unto him with his disciples also, he said unto them, whosoever will come after me, let him deny himself, and take up his cross, and follow me. For whosoever will save his life shall lose it; but whosoever shall lose his life for my sake and the gospel's, the same shall save it.

He told us, "Verily, verily except a man be born of water and of the Spirit, he cannot enter into the kingdom of God. That which is born of the flesh is flesh; and that which is born of the Spirit is spirit." In Jesus' baptism he fulfilled all righteousness and the Holy Ghost came upon him. He had told us in scripture that God would put a new heart and his own Spirit within us. This was called God's work and the operation of God and by faith it would in a nno second, the Spirit of truth will quicken us into Christ. Know you not, that so many of us as were baptized into Jesus Christ were baptized into his death. Therefore we are buried with him in baptism into death: that like as Christ was raised up from the dead by the glory of the Father, even so we should walk in new life. Knowing this, that our old man is crucified with him, that the body of sin might be destroyed, that henceforth we should not serve sin. For sin shall not have dominion over us for we are not under the law, but under grace. We would come up out of the water a *new Creature* in *Christ* and the Holy Ghost will come upon you. The Spirit of truth in us is his same spirit that Jesus gave to his Father on the cross (*Father into thy hands I commend my spirit*). *All new Creatures in Christ* are members of the body of Christ, who all have the same Spirit of truth within them.

I am crucified with Christ: nevertheless I live; yet not I, but Christ lives in me: and the life which I now live in the flesh I live by the faith of the Son of God, who loved me, and gave himself for me (Galatians 2:20).

Jesus said, I am the way, the truth, and the life: no man comes unto the Father, but by me.

Read the "Gospel of John" the Apostle that Jesus loved because he believed him and came to know him. We all need to come to know Jesus so we know who we are in Christ.

1. Luke 8:11-15, Mark 4:14-20, Matthew 13: 18-23:
    When God gives a parable three times there is something good in all three.

    The sower and the seed parable mainly showed the four hearts of men. They had all heard the Gospel but their hearts reacted differently to it. *Unless* numbers one through three get ready for when Jesus returns, they will be left behind and then seriously will have to choose to die for Jesus at the hands of the enemy. Then they will receive their new lives in the second chance of the millennium.

    The fourth ones who are the members of the body of Christ (*new Creatures*) must remain ready, always helping the lost to believe the Gospel and become saved and make them disciples before the "Christ Creature Air Express" comes.

    We are God's living temple (building) Jesus is the only foundation. Let every man take heed how he builds thereupon it. Every mans work shall be made manifest: for the day shall declare it. Because it shall be revealed by fire; and the fire shall try every mans work of what sort it is. If any man's work abide which he has built thereupon, he shall receive a reward. If any man's work shall be burned, he shall suffer loss: but he himself shall be saved; yet so as by fire.

    Once you are this far, read from Romans to Philemon and I John. If there is still time; by now you *are* one of *the fourth in the parable* and can understand, so now try the Revelation of Jesus Christ to St John.

    (I pray for all those who have believed the words that came from Gods Book, the King James Bible 1611 that is 401 years old. Man has not changed it. Everything was arranged in his book to give understanding to those who love God or want to learn to love this awesome, wonderful, magnificent, faithful God, who is love himself and was gracious to share it all with of us who came out of the darkness and into the light. Thanks be to the God of our Lord Jesus Christ, the Father of glory who is the light of the world and now he shines through Christ in us. God bless you all and thank you for reading the book. May the love of God draw you near and let your hearts not be troubled. Amen.)

REFERENCES

Chapter 1—Genesis 1-8

Chapter 2—Genesis 9-11

Chapter 3—Genesis 11-21

Chapter 4—Genesis 37-50

Chapter 5—Exodus 2-14

Chapter 6—Exodus 14-34

Chapter 7—Hebrews 1; 1 Kings 5; Psalms 45; Genesis 38; Isaiah 44; Ezra 6; Haggai 1; 1 Corinthians; Luke 6-14; Acts 17; Revelations 21

Chapter 8—1 Peter; John 19; 1 Kings; 2 Kings

Chapter 9—Hebrews 8; Galatians 4; Isaiah 7; Luke 1; Luke 2; Matthew 2; Luke 11

Chapter 10—Genesis; Isaiah 28

Chapter 11—Luke 3-23; Matthew 3-27; Mark 1; John 3-18; Ezekiel 18; Colossians 1

Chapter 12—Genesis, Luke, Isaiah, Matthew, Mark, Hebrews, 1 Peter, John, Acts

Chapter 13—John 17